"Telling Florida Tales with Delight, Gusto..."
"A pioneer died 'after being kicked in the head by a mule.' Century-old oak trees have branches which 'extend so far that the lower ones droop to rest an elbow on the ground.' That's the way Nixon Smiley gives readers the setting and action of 18 stories of real places and real people. The book is easy reading. It's the sort of book one would put beside a favorite chair to pick up and dip into while nibbling a handful of chocolates or sipping a nightcap. . . . Readers who have never visited Florida may get the most from the book. They can soak up Florida lore while 'seeing' the state through Nixon Smiley's observant eyes. The author writes with gusto of colorful personalities. His latest book will bring special satisfaction to his fans because the first chapter tells a little about him and his boyhood on the St. Johns River. . . . The same bold and vivid feeling, the glare of sunlight that illumines Florida, is conveyed by the illustrations, drawings by Bob Lamme." *MIAMI HERALD*

FLORIDA
Land of Images

BY NIXON SMILEY

with drawings by Bob Lamme

E. A. SEEMANN PUBLISHING, INC.
Miami, Florida

To Evelyn, my wife

Contents

Introduction

*

While writing these stories about unusual places in Florida and about some of the more colorful people who have played roles in its history, it occurred to me that they could be arranged in the order that a motorist might travel conveniently through the state. And so I laid out the stories to follow one another in succession, from north to south along the east coast, to Key West, then partway up the Gulf coast, and ending in central and north Florida. I discovered that this is also a convenient arrangement from the standpoint of history.

This is not meant to be a guide to Florida, however, listing and discussing the countless attractions, natural and fabricated, announced in neon hues wherever the motorist goes throughout the state. There already are many tour guides to Florida, together with maps and countless brochures describing individual attractions. Travel agencies can obtain information on such attractions as Walt Disney World and the public tours at the John F. Kennedy Space Center. Automobile associations can supply tour routes of the state. And information about local tourist attractions can be obtained by writing to chambers of commerce in most Florida communities of any size.

I have limited my stories to the Florida peninsula. The western part of Florida—Madison, Monticello, Tallahassee, Marianna, Panama City, and Pensacola—is vastly different from the rest of the state in many ways. Although the state capital is at Tallahassee, the history of west Florida is in many ways more closely allied with southern Alabama and southern Georgia than with the peninsula.

The eighteen titles in this volume are built around real places and real people, together with my impressions retained after nearly a quarter-century of traveling about the state and writing for *The Miami Herald.* If I have written with enthusiasm it is because I have enjoyed my experiences in seeking out the interesting and picturesque and writing about them for newspaper readers. I took the view that most *Herald* readers would never see the places I wrote about, and I sought to take them to the scenes and share with them what I saw and felt. This book I have written with the same feeling.

Miami, 1972   Nixon Smiley

FLORIDA: Land of Images

Land of Images

To countless millions, Florida is a land of images.

Every visitor carries home a dominant mental picture of what the state is like. That picture might be the beach at Key Biscayne against a background of coconut palms, or the thrilling experience of playing a tarpon in the mangrove-covered Ten Thousand Islands; driving through the rolling hills of central Florida in January when the citrus groves are covered with colorful oranges, or watching the fishes cavort in the unbelievably clear water of a Florida spring; or, for the very lucky, seeing the earth-shaking departure of a Saturn rocket from its pad at the John F. Kennedy Space Center, on its way to the moon. For a child the image of Florida might begin and end at Walt Disney World, with its fantastic numbers of lively mechanical creatures and its unforgettable rides. For the unfortunate who spends a vacation in Florida during bad weather, the image is likely to be anything but pleasant —of cloudy, rainy days, cold nights, perhaps a wind out of the northeast which drives everything off the beaches except the gulls and sandpipers. And, of course, there are the hurricanes. Yet, while these great storms may threaten Florida nearly every year during the hurricane season, from June to the end of October, they seldom hit. If they did, Florida would hardly be a popular place to live. But the visitor who rides out a Florida hurricane in a resort hotel returns home with more to talk about than he would have after ten ordinary vacations. And the day he rode out a hurricane—in Key West, Miami, West Palm Beach, Fort Myers, or wherever— probably would be forever a dominant image of Florida.

The first recorded impression of Florida was that of Ponce de León, who, on his first voyage in 1513, noted the "many . . . cool woodlands." Because Ponce landed on Easter, the day the Feast of Flowers *(Pascua florida)* was being celebrated in Spain, he named the land La Florida. In his report to King Charles V, Ponce made no mention of the new territory being a "land of flowers," as some promoters suggest. His image of Florida was one of "cool woodlands." Had Ponce landed in August instead of March he might have departed with a different image. His image was much different after his second voyage in 1521, when he was wounded by an Indian arrow, from which he later died.

My earliest image of Florida is a picture of the broad Saint Johns River, on whose shore, at Orange Park, I was born in 1911. I remember, as a child, of being on a steamboat from which I saw giant live oaks which reached out from the banks to dip their moss-laden branches into the quiet, dark surface. And I remember the boat approaching and being tied up to a wharf that extended far out into the river. Although I departed from the river while quite young, this image remained in my mind long after I was grown. But after moving to Miami in 1935, where I have lived since, that early image was replaced by another. When I was in the Pacific during World War II the picture that dominated my memory was Biscayne Boulevard, with its islands of royal palms, with the city of Miami on one side and Bayfront Park on the other. Sometimes a picture of the Everglades, with the endless saw grass and willow clumps marking alligator holes, intruded. But the picture of Biscayne Boulevard dominated. This scene had been so striking to me upon seeing Miami for the first time, when in all of Dade County there were not quite 200,000 people. If I were to leave Miami today and stay away for a time, I'm not sure what mental image of Florida would become dominant in my mind. I'm afraid it might be confused. Any city that has grown as rapidly as Miami is likely to create confusion in one's mind. And, yet, Miami has grown into one of the most interesting cities of the world, with an international flavor; a city with liberalism along with great wealth, and rare tolerance; a city of creative talent, resulting in an immense cultural impetus. It is an activist city where the traffic is fast and the competition keen. Miami has attracted a great many colorful personalities, from hippies to multimillionaires, who play roles in a wide variety of activities. *The Miami Herald* has become one of the most popular newspapers in America for young newspapermen who want to work in a city where "everything" happens, where virtually all the great and near-great are moving in and out constantly. I wouldn't want to leave Miami, but should I do so the dominating image I would take with me certainly would not be Biscayne Boulevard, with its heavy traffic and parked automobiles among the palms. No, the image would not be of downtown at all, but probably a picture of my five acres of pinewoods and palmettos about a pond on the outskirts of Miami, where at dusk—at martini time—a score or more of wild wood ducks plunge from the fading sky to splash down in the dark water, to spend the night in a little wild oasis surrounded by urban development.

Certainly I would entertain no dominant image of the Saint Johns, whose water is so polluted that many years and countless millions of dollars will be needed to clean it up. But the old image of the Saint Johns comes to mind whenever I hear the tone poem, *Florida Suite,* composed by Frederick Delius. Delius was twenty-two when his father, a Bradford, England, textile manufacturer, sent him to Florida in 1884 to manage an orange grove at Picolata, on the eastern shore of the Saint Johns below Mandarin. The elder Delius hoped the experience in the Florida wilderness would turn his son's mind away from an infatuation with music, maturing him and hardening him for a career in the textile business. But the Florida experience had the opposite effect. The picturesque river with its multitude of wildlife, the primitive landscape with its strange birdsongs and new smells formed indelible images in the mind of the sensitive young man. Moreover, there were the friendly black people, including Elbert Anderson and his wife, Eliza, who lived on the property. They introduced Delius to a world he would never have known in Europe. But to cap it off, Delius found Jacksonville, a few hours by steamboat from Picolata, to be more of a center of culture than his hometown of Bradford. There he found a master teacher of music, Thomas Ward, whom Delius would remember in old age as the only teacher who ever taught him anything. Two years later when Delius departed from the Saint Johns his career was set. Instead of returning to Bradford, he went to Germany where he began in earnest the career of composer. But the sights and the sounds of the Saint Johns were not forgotten, and Delius was soon working on a music composition that expressed his image of the river, its scenery, its wildlife, its people, particularly the black people. The four movements of the *Florida Suite*—Daybreak, By the River, Sunset, At Night—record impressions of the Saint Johns which must have been shared by thousands of those early Florida tourists who remembered the river when it was one of America's most popular and fascinating vacation spots. The small cottage in which Delius lived at Picolata has been moved to Jacksonville University and restored.

The modern visitor to Florida would hardly think of the Saint Johns River as a tourist attraction, and certainly no visitor would consider any of the cities or towns along the river as winter resorts. Today it is south Florida—Palm Beach, Fort Lauderdale, Miami, Clearwater, Saint Petersburg, Sarasota, Naples—which fits the image. But for a quarter-century after the Civil War it was north Florida that attracted the visitors—the Saint Johns River with its invitation to adventure, and old Saint Augustine with its relics of Spanish occupation.

Jacksonville was for a time the most important tourist destination in Florida. That was because Jacksonville, a seaport and a river port, as well as an important railway terminal, was a jumping-off place for steamboat trips up the Saint Johns. Resort towns sprang up along the river all the way to Sanford—Orange Park, Mandarin, Green Cove Springs, Tocoi, Palatka, Enterprise, Sanford. The trips upriver were popular because of the abundant wildlife—ducks, wading birds, alligators—against a primitive background of forest and of orange groves along the shore. As a steamboat plied its way through the quiet water of the broad river, thousands of ducks rose from the surface, while herons, ibises, roseate spoonbills, even flamingoes, took flight from sandbars and shallow areas beyond the channel. And alligators of all sizes slid off sandbars where they had been sunning. Sportsmen lined the decks of the steamboats to fire at the wildlife. The sport was altogether for the marksmanship. Nothing was recovered. The dead and crippled birds and alligators were left behind as the men reloaded their guns and readied themselves for the next chance to fire at some hapless wild thing. From descriptions left by travelers of that period and recounted in such magazines as *Scribners* and *Harpers,* the wildlife on the

Saint Johns was so prolific that the prospect of killing if off hardly seemed possible.

Harriet Beecher Stowe, who had a winter home at Mandarin, sought to stop the senseless slaughter. But while the author of *Uncle Tom's Cabin* may have planted the seeds of disapproval in a few minds, her criticisms failed to stop the brutal and pointless warfare against nature. The word "conservation," in its present meaning, had not been invented. There is no evidence that Mrs. Stowe reached the conscience or the intellect of business-minded boat owners and resort operators who advertised and promoted the river trips for the sights and the shooting. An engraving appearing in *Scribner's* in 1874 shows sportsmen firing at alligators from a steamboat, as fashionably clad women, displaying Victorian era feminine sensitivity, hold their fingers in their ears and look the other way to avoid sound and sight of the slaughter.

Many notable travelers came in the 1870s and 1880s, including Presidents Ulysses S. Grant and Grover Cleveland. The latter selected the Saint Johns for a honeymoon. Mrs. Stowe arrived shortly after the Civil War, but as a winter resident rather than a short-time visitor. She settled her family first at Orange Park, then discovered Mandarin. Other visitors to the Saint Johns during those years included General Robert E. Lee, Sidney Lanier, William Cullen Bryant, and Baron Frederick de Bary. The baron purchased a large tract on the Saint Johns on Lake Monroe, near Enterprise, and built a home where he entertained in lavish European style. The house still stands, in the town named after him, DeBary, and is maintained and kept open for the public by the state of Florida.

Mrs. Stowe, Lanier, and Bryant were among America's notable writers during the 1800s, and the glowing accounts they wrote of the Saint Johns, as well as its tributary, the Oklawaha, and Silver Springs, were widely read. Mrs. Stowe's *Palmetto Leaves,* mainly an account of her experiences and observations on the Saint Johns, brought tens of thousands of visitors to Florida. Mrs. Stowe and her husband, Dr. Calvin Stowe, an Episcopalian minister, spent their winters in Mandarin from 1868 until 1884. They built a gingerbread-fringed cottage that resembled a cross between a New England barn, a Southern plantation dwelling, and a cathedral without steeples. It stood beneath huge live oaks—oaks that are still standing. A photograph shows the porch built around one of the monstrous oaks.

Because Mandarin was the home of America's best-known writer, it was a favorite steamboat pause. The curious hoped to get a glimpse of Mrs. Stowe, and there is a legend still alive in Mandarin that she received a fee from the steamboat owners to sit on the porch of her cottage so the eager passengers could see her. In the early years the Stowes had been safe from the curious. There was no suitable place for the bigger boats to dock and they merely passed offshore, close enough for the passengers to see the Stowe cottage and one or both of the Stowes sitting on the porch. More frequently it was the Reverend Mr. Stowe, who resembled Charles Darwin, wearing a red skull cap to hide his bald head. If Mrs. Stowe wasn't visible she probably was writing, for she was in constant need of funds to maintain her Florida property, her northern property, and her family.

Then in 1878, a pier, complete with passenger terminal and docking facilities for big steamboats, was built on the river almost next door to the Stowe cottage. It was quite a dock, 556 feet long, extending to deep water. The Stowes no longer were safe. Passengers poured from the steamers, ran from the pier and invaded the Stowe property. They not only plucked the oranges from the trees, but grabbed Mrs. Stowe's blouses from the clotheslines. One can imagine the scene. The distraught Stowe employees were not equal to their responsibilities of protecting the property, even when armed with brooms and sticks. The Stowes hastily retreated inside,

where they locked themselves in from the fury of the invaders. The Stowes made their final trip to Florida during the
winter of 1883-84. Their cottage disappeared years ago, the
lumber being carried off by the local people, and another
house now occupies the site beheath the live oaks on the
Saint Johns.

About the time the Stowes were departing for the last time,
a new and influential book, *Florida For Tourists, Invalids,
and Settlers,* by George Barbour, was becoming a best seller.
Barbour, who described the scenery, the climate, the economy, and the "clay-eating" Crackers, not only attracted
thousands of visitors to Florida, but countless settlers.

Jacksonville, hardly more than a village at the end of the
Civil War, was by 1880 a city of 18,000, but more than
doubled its population during the winter. It had three luxury
resort hotels, the Carlton House, the St. James and the Windsor, and numerous smaller hotels and boarding houses. In the
major hotels, built around Hemming Park, the Continental
waiters spoke French as well as English. The big hotels
boasted their own orchestras, while the city of Jacksonville,
which claimed to be the "cultural capital of Florida," maintained a full symphony orchestra and an opera house. Other
resort hotels flourished in towns along the Saint Johns, including Silver Springs, up the Oklawaha.

The trip up the Oklawaha, a tortuously winding, narrow
stream through a jungle that hid the banks on either side, was
usually made at night. The steamboat left Palatka in the middle afternoon, reaching the mouth of the Oklawaha by dusk
on a short winter day. Navigating the snaked-shaped Oklawaha required familarity not only with the riverbed, but even
with the trees hanging over the swift stream. The busy helms-
man guided his steamboat with the aid of firelight made by
burning rich pine in a metal box off the bridge. The eerie
lights and shadows, the screams of disturbed wildlife, the red
glows of hundreds of alligator eyes, and the hooting of owls

in the jungle fastness made the trip an exciting one. Just as unforgettable was Silver Springs, from whose mysterious caverns boiled more than half a billion gallons of crystal-clear water a day. The steamboat reached the springs in time for breakfast in the Silver Springs Hotel.

Still another adventure remained for tourists who were of strong constitution and able to withstand hardships. That was a journey by steamboat up the Saint Johns beyond Enterprise and Sanford, to Salt Lake, for an eight-mile overland trip to Titusville in a mule-drawn railway car. George Barbour, recounting his experiences on this trip, noted that upstream to Salt Lake was a distance of 311 miles by boat from Jacksonville, although only 145 miles in a direct line.

Titus House, the travelers' destination, was operated by Colonel Henry Titus, who had made history before the Civil War as the principal political and military antagonist of John Brown in Kansas, before Brown's capture at Harper's Ferry. But while Titus was a colorful personality that travelers enjoyed, what really attracted them to Titusville was the fishing and the hunting, the Indian River oysters, and the steaks from green turtles captured on the ocean beaches. No relics remain of that era, but motoring along Indian River Drive, which winds through the cabbage palms and oaks along the waterfront, takes you back to a more relaxed period before the building of an "earthport" on Merritt Island, across Indian River from Titusville, for trips to the moon and the planets.

Not all visitors to the Saint Johns could afford to stay in the luxury resort hotels, and the local residents took advantage of this by opening their homes to boarders. My maternal grandparents, Mr. and Mrs. N. J. Strickland, came from Dublin, Georgia, to Orange Park in the 1880s and built a large residence which they turned into a boarding house. Among their boarders were John Burroughs, the naturalist, and Nixon Waterman, onetime newspaperman, poet, and Chau-

tauqua lecturer. By the turn of the century the Saint Johns
had lost its appeal, the wildlife having been decimated, while
Ormond, Palm Beach, Miami, and Saint Petersburg were at-
tracting most of the winter visitors, particularly the rich and
fashionable. But a few visitors, including Burroughs and
Waterman, kept coming long after the riverboats ceased to
steam out from Jacksonville with their decks filled with
armed sportsmen and their gorgeously dressed ladies for trips
up the Saint Johns.

No, I never had the opportunity to see either Burroughs or
Waterman at Orange Park. But I did get Waterman's first
name, and came close to getting Burroughs' too. My mother,
an admirer of both men, whom she had known since a girl,
wanted to name her first child, if a boy, for them. But by
which name would he be called? The two men settled the
problem by tossing a coin. Nixon Waterman won. The way
the coin fell was to have an immense influence on my life,
although I was not to see Mr. Waterman until I was seventeen. Having lost both parents by the time I was seven, I
spent most of my young life with my paternal grandparents
in Crowder, a Deep South farm community near the Florida-
Georgia line. But during those formative years Nixon Waterman was to me a very great man, and I dreamed of being,
somehow, like him after I grew up. The year I was seventeen
I was invited to Canton, Massachusetts, to spend several weeks
with Mr. and Mrs. Waterman. While I was there Mr. Waterman
recounted his experiences as a newspaper writer and editor.
The stories he told were thrilling to me and made me want
more than ever to be a newspaperman, but lacking in education and training, such a career seemed remote. Five years
later, however, I got a job as a copy boy on the *Florida
Times-Union* in Jacksonville, a job which proved to be the
beginning of a newspaper career at least as colorful and as
interesting as Nixon Waterman could claim.

But where one visitor, Nixon Waterman, may have left his

influence on one Floridian, another visitor was to influence millions. He was Henry M. Flagler, partner of John D. and William Rockefeller in the building of the Standard Oil empire. Flagler came to Jacksonville in December of 1883 on a honeymoon with his second wife, Alice Shourds. After a few days at the luxurious St. James, the Flaglers took a steamboat trip up the Saint Johns to Green Cove Springs. Although no sportsman, Flagler did enjoy the scenery, and he particularly enjoyed picking oranges from a grove at Tocoi, across the river from Green Cove. But one day on the river was enough; and Flagler also had enough of Jacksonville. So the Flaglers checked out from the St. James, returned to Tocoi, and boarded a train for a 15-mile trip to Saint Augustine. It turned out to be one of the most portentous occurrences for Florida since the settlement of Saint Augustine by Pedro Menéndez 400 years before.

What is left on the Saint Johns for visitors to see which might be reminiscent of that period when this colorful river was tourist destination number one? Hardly anything, except for the moss-laden live oaks, the cabbage palms, and the magnolias along the shores. Even the citrus groves are gone, the trees having been killed in two severe freezes which hit Florida during the winter of 1894-95. As a result of those freezes, Mrs. Julia Tuttle, who owned one of the three houses on the Miami River at that time, induced Flagler to extend his railroad to Biscayne Bay and create the city of Miami. In the meantime the Saint Johns acquired the infamous water hyacinth, a floating plant whose flower resembles that of the true hyacinth. The Saint Johns' equally infamous little old lady, Mrs. W. F. Fuller of Palatka, in 1884 attended the Pan American Exposition at New Orleans, where she bought a "beautiful" floating water plant from Venezuela. The plant proliferated in her garden pool, and when Mrs. Fuller noted the attractive purple flowers she began calling her plant a "water hyacinth." In time her pool became crowded with the plants. Although she gave plants to her friends, her pool was soon crowded again. Mrs. Fuller dumped the excess plants into the Saint Johns, which flowed past her garden. By the time Mrs. Fuller's "lovely" plant was recognized as a menace to navigation, to fishing, to wildlife, and even to the aesthetics of the Saint Johns, it was too late. Eradication is now deemed impossible, and millions of dollars must be spent each year by state and federal agencies for the control of the hyacinth, since spread to lakes and streams throughout the state.

But while the hyacinth has proliferated, the resort hotels along the Saint Johns have disappeared. The ornate structures were abandoned after the tourists stopped coming, and the natives carried away the furnishings, the lumber, and the timbers piece by piece. At Enterprise it wasn't just the hotel that the natives carried away; they carried away the whole town. Where the lavish Brock House stood among the giant live oaks on Lake Monroe's waterfront, only the rotting pilings of the old wharf, where steamboats tied up, remain to remind you of that fabulous period. Once a thriving community and the seat of Mosquito County (since changed to Volusia), Enterprise became a ghost town. Only the graveyard, house foundations, brick streets, and the live oaks survived. A children's home now occupies the grounds of the Brock House, surrounded by those centuries-old oaks whose branches extend so far that the lower ones droop to rest an elbow on the ground. Modest concrete block houses and azalea gardens line the old streets.

Palatka became a major sawmill town after the tourists departed. Centuries-old cypresses in the Oklawaha valley and in the upper reaches of the Saint Johns were cut and rafted downstream to Palatka. The thriving town boasted several millionaires. A new downtown was built, the red-brick streets extended to accommodate a fashionable residential section along the river. After cutting the timber, Palatka's million-

aires departed, taking their money with them, and the community became so depressed it was for a time in danger of
becoming a ghost town, like Enterprise. But the Hudson Pulp
& Paper Co. built a huge mill here after World War II, reviving
the economy, although at the cost of fouling the air. Driving
through the old residential sections of Palatka today you can
see how the affluent lived during Palatka's better days, in fine
homes behind massive moss-laden oaks, magnolias, and hickories. But many of the old homes have been converted into
apartment houses, while brick streets have been covered with
asphalt. Most of Palatka's citizens you talk with have never
heard of that glorious period when it was one of the principal
resorts on the Saint Johns south of Jacksonville, entertaining
President Ulysses S. Grant and President Grover Cleveland.
Most outsiders today know Palatka principally for its famous
azalea Ravine Gardens, developed by the Works Progress Administration (WPA), during the depression of the 1930s. Now
a state park, the eighty-five-acre garden, in the ravine of a
creek emptying into the Saint Johns, is surrounded by a five-
mile loop drive. Thousands visit the gardens during azalea
flowering time in late February and March.

For those who enjoy old churches, Palatka has one that
should not be missed. It is St. Marks Episcopal Church, designed by Richard Upjohn, whose Trinity Church in New
York City is so well known. It also is one of Florida's oldest
church buildings, having been erected in 1850. But there are
other interesting churches along the Saint Johns, at Orange
Park, Hibernia, Green Cove Springs, and Mandarin. It is a
remarkable coincidence that all of these churches are Episcopal, and to a large extent most of them are along the style of
Upjohn's churches, except the Episcopal Church of Our
Savior at Mandarin. The Mandarin church became nationally
known half a century ago when black children raised a fund,
through penny and nickel donations, to install a stained glass
window in the memory of Harriet Beecher Stowe.

Mrs. Stowe had contributed to the building of the little church in the early 1880s while living at Mandarin. Of Elizabethan style, the church stood on the shore above the Saint Johns, its peaked and shingled belfry resembling a gingerbread-fringed watchtower. Shortly after Mrs. Stowe lost her husband in 1886, she wrote from Connecticut asking that the end window be reserved for a stained glass memorial in honor of Dr. Stowe. But the window failed to arrive during her lifetime. With advancing age and decline of health, Mrs. Stowe no longer could turn out the voluminous writings which had supported her and her family. Meanwhile, the other windows received stained glass, but the largest window, behind the altar and facing the river, was reserved, even after Mrs. Stowe's death in 1896. A nationwide subscription to raise funds for the window was begun in 1913. The window, depicting a great live oak, "symbol of the Stowes' love of Mandarin," was completed in 1916 by Louis Tiffany.

The Episcopal Church of Our Savior became a shrine for admirers of the author of *Uncle Tom's Cabin.* After the steamboats stopped running, automobiles brought visitors, down Mandarin Avenue beneath some of the largest live oaks in Florida, to the quaint church framed by oaks and hickories. The unique architecture and the beauty of its stained glass windows, particularly the Tiffany window, made it for a time one of the most popular tourist attractions in Florida. Then, in the fall of 1965, Hurricane Dora passed over Mandarin during the night. Next morning the church was found smashed by a giant hickory. Chopping through the foliage, townspeople discovered that all but one of the stained glass windows had miraculously escaped damage. But the Stowe memorial lay scattered in thousands of pieces. Like the church, there was no hope of restoring it.

A new and larger church was built on the site, but not until members settled a disagreement over the design. The younger people wanted a large, modern church; the old church had been too small. The older people wanted the destroyed church replaced exactly as it was. Eventually there was a compromise. The new structure was built large enough for the needs of the community, while at one end a chapel duplicating the original church was built. In the chapel were placed the recovered stained glass windows, all dedicated to children or to spouses who died long ago.

Visiting the church after its completion, I was impressed by the architect's success in the welding of the old and the new. And one can hardly study the fine old windows, which in a few years will pass the century mark, without contemplating the singular development in the human species—a conscience that makes us create memorials to those we are devoted to, whether a child, a spouse, or a talented individual.

For the "collector" of unique churches that have pleasing design, atmosphere, and a story, none in Florida surpasses St. Margaret's Episcopal Church at Hibernia, on the Saint Johns between Orange Park and Green Cove Springs. Hibernia is not included on most road maps, and, after a rain, the sand and clay road that gets you to the church may be anything but inviting. But if you can find Hibernia, and you do get there, the gem at the end of the road is well worth the trouble.

St. Margaret's is a postage-stamp size church, hidden in a wilderness. It's the quietness that gets to you first, then the church. The stained glass windows, the board-and-batten siding, the sharply pitched roof, the cupola on top, all framed by the branches of an ancient live oak, take you into the past. The quieting effect is immediate. As you study the church you don't have to be Episcopalian—you don't have to be religious at all—to feel the influence of that indefinable search by man for some kind of spiritual satisfaction. The slender chimney tells you something else about man: he wants comfort while searching for those spiritual ends. But the cylinders of natural gas that stand at one corner of the building tell you more: that modern man wants his comfort

instantly and completely, which a wood fire could hardly
provide on a frigid Sunday morning.

You open the unlocked gate to the churchyard with some
trepidation, walk around the building, discover a cemetery
among the trees and scrub. You think, well, if you've got to
go, if you've got to be buried someplace, this would be preferable to the cleanly-mowed, characterless modern cemetery. But today you are alive, and you can walk through the
cemetery and study the gravestones and wonder about the
people who were buried here long ago.

The cemetery antedates the church. It was begun in 1821
with the burial of George Fleming, founder of Hibernia Plantation. Fleming was Irish, born in 1760. He came to Florida
in his twenties, obtaining from the Spanish a 1,000-acre grant
of land on the Saint Johns. He named his plantation Hibernia, Latin for Ireland. Across the river lived Francisco
Philip Fatio, a wealthy Spaniard who had seven daughters.
Fleming courted and married Sophia Felipina Fatio. Their
grandson, Francis Philip Fleming, would serve as Florida's
twenty-first governor, 1889-1893. The graves of "George
Fleming, 1760-1821 [and] His Wife, Sophia Fatio, 1765-1848,"
are marked by a single headstone.

A son, Lewis Fleming, who would sire a governor of Florida, became the owner of Hibernia. He married Margaret
Seton, an Episcopalian, who, like his mother, also lived
"across the river." Margaret, surviving her husband, built the
Hibernia church in 1875. But because the family had been
impoverished by the Civil War, only the walls and the roof
were immediately completed. In 1877 yellow fever hit Jacksonville, and Margaret sent a daughter, Maggie, her namesake,
to help nurse a son and his family. But it was Maggie who
died. The body, sealed in a lead casket, was transported from
Jacksonville to Hibernia by river steamer. Blaming herself for
the death of Maggie, the mother lived but a few months, in
the meantime rushing completion of the church. And today

you find the gravestones of two Margaret Flemings in Hibernia cemetery—Margaret Fleming, 1813-1878, and Margaret Fleming, 1852-1877—mother and daughter. Little imagination is needed to suggest how St. Margaret's Episcopal Church got its name.

But while churches and cemeteries have survived as landmarks of the Saint Johns' past, little else remains. In Green Cove Springs, only a name, Saratoga Street, and the spring itself remain as reminders of the nineteenth century. It originally was known as White Spring, because of a single spring from which flowed 3,000 gallons of sulfurous-smelling water every minute. Promoters built a hotel facing the spring, the Clarendon, and renamed the resort Green Cove Springs, after postal authorities refused to approve the name of Saratoga Springs because of possible confusion with Saratoga Springs, New York. Green Cove's mineral springs became famous for a time. Invalids—rheumatics, the crippled, aged, and infirm—swore they felt better after immersing themselves in the seventy-eight-degree water and drenching their gullets with the bad-tasting minerals. They felt strong enough to attend the horse races in the afternoon on Saratoga Street. And, in the evening, after wining and dining themselves in the Clarendon's luxurious dining room, they felt good enough to stay up late hours placing bets in the hotel's casino.

The Clarendon burned early in this century, and in its place was built the Qui-Si-Sana Hotel, named after a then-famous hotel in Italy. But by that time interest in the Saint Johns had passed. Only the invalids and oldsters who had discovered Green Cove at an earlier period kept returning to enjoy the imagined miracle of the spring. The Qui-Si-Sana, its name now changed to Green Cove Motor Inn, still stands facing Saratoga Street and the spring, whose warm water flows from an unimaginatively built concrete enclosure into a municipally-owned swimming pool. A gate to the high chain-link fence surrounding the pool is kept locked in winter.

In late 1971, while doing a story on Green Cove Springs for *The Miami Herald,* I dropped in at the hotel to get some background. A young woman in the office was unable to help, having been on the job only a couple of weeks, but as I was about to depart she recalled a complaint from a guest she thought was interesting and funny. The guest, an elderly woman, had registered at the hotel with her family to spend a night. But when she discovered that the swimming pool was closed, she expressed disappointment.

"The pool was open throughout the winter when I used to stay here," said the guest, who, unable to relive the pleasant memory of a time when Green Cove was still a lively resort, probably would return no more.

Jacksonville's famous resort hotels burned in 1901, when a fire leveled 130 blocks, virtually all of the city. In central downtown only a Confederate monument, a soldier standing atop a tall column in Hemming Park, survived. The soldier still stands there in the same pose, as if half-heartedly guarding the city. He must have gotten plenty hot when the massive wooden St. James and Windsor Hotels, which faced Hemming Park, burned. A new Windsor was built, but failed to recapture the glory of the past. It was later dismantled and today a ten-cent store occupies the site. A department store occupies the site of the old St. James.

Some claim, incorrectly, that Jacksonville's impressive railway terminal, at Bay and Lee Streets, escaped the fire. This terminal, however, was built in 1919. It was the old terminal, built in 1895, that escaped the fire. It still stands, housing the offices of the Jacksonville Terminal Company, organized by Flagler. The old building, which faces Bay Street next door to the present terminal, shows the influence of the Moorish-Spanish design that went into Flagler's Ponce de Leon Hotel at Saint Augustine, which he built in the 1880s. The older structure is overshadowed by the 1919 terminal, which is still today one of Jacksonville's impressive buildings. Whenever I pass the building, its entrance set off by fourteen magnificent sandstone columns that rise the equivalent of three stories, I cannot help feeling a nostalgia for the day when it was the busiest passenger terminal in Florida, when thousands of people crowded day and night through its huge vaulted waiting room, its dome soaring to seventy feet. That was before the development of electronic broadcast systems, when the live voices of the red-capped announcers reverberated about the huge building as they called out the arrival or departure of trains, genuinely impressing a country boy from Crowder.

After giving up its title as the state's tourist capital, Jacksonville for years called itself the Gateway City to Florida. The opening of modern highway systems and the development of air travel made this claim no longer valid. For a time Jacksonville promoted itself as "Florida's Industrial City." A thriving seaport was developed, together with shipbuilding, and Jacksonville's leaders offered both the river and the air to polluting industries. The river became virtually a cesspool, while its decaying waterfront was one of Florida's greatest eyesores. The air stank from the smoke of pulp mills while soot from the cheap oils burned in the city-owned power plants blanketed the city. But in the 1960s the people of Jacksonville turned again toward the river and rediscovered something long forgotten—that the Saint Johns could be beautiful. The decaying wharves and abandoned shipbuilding yards were dismantled, new buildings and parks constructed along the waterfront. In the meantime, the voters turned out the old politicians and installed new leaders who promised to clean up the air and the Saint Johns. Today Jacksonville is, from the air, one of Florida's most attractive cities. But that beauty is dependent on the Saint Johns, to which Jacksonville's finest residential areas as well as its business section are oriented.

For the average visitor to Florida, hastening down a high-speed throughway to Walt Disney World at Orlando, or to one of the resorts farther south, there is today disappointingly little to see in Jacksonville that cannot be seen back home. It seems to be just another city, better seen from Interstate-95 as it crosses the Saint Johns than at close range. There also is little to see on the Saint Johns. The abundant wildlife is gone, along with the steamboats, and few relics recalling the river's colorful past have survived. Yet, neither Jacksonville nor the river should be discounted by those who are fortunate to possess a feeling for history, who have enough sense of humor to like a good story, and who, with little strain on the imagination, can repopulate a once lively scene with those active, colorful personalities who lived long ago. There was something about the Saint Johns that attracted a considerable number of restless, enterprising, and interesting people, beginning with the French Huguenots who built Fort Caroline on the river in 1564.

Every schoolchild knows the story of the Huguenot massacre by the Spanish under Conquistador Pedro Menéndez in 1565. The National Park Service has built a replica of Fort Caroline on the south side of the Saint Johns between Jacksonville and the car ferry crossing at Mayport. A museum tells the story of the destruction of the French colony by the Spanish, who claimed Florida as a possession. The attempt by the French to colonize Florida led to the founding of Saint Augustine, a military outpost to protect the Spanish empire in America from further encroachment by European powers. But that is part of the Saint Augustine story. First belongs the story about three incredible individuals of the Saint Johns—Captain John McQueen, Revolutionary War veteran and confidante of George Washington; John Houstoun McIntosh, president of the East Florida Republic, and Zephaniah Kingsley, slave trader, keeper of a black harem, collector of human scalps, master of international intrigue. Moreover, the houses in which these men lived, on Fort George Sound, a tributary of the Saint Johns, still stand. These two structures, which have miraculously escaped destruction by decay or fire, two hazards which have destroyed most of Florida's relics not built of stone, are now owned by the state of Florida, which maintains them and keeps them open to the public for a small fee.

BOB LAMME

TWO

Three Incredible Adventurers

Like all wars, the American Revolutionary War produced many discontent and restless men who, after the conflict was over, found it difficult to return to the humdrum of everyday life. Among them was John McQueen, South Carolina plantation owner, a captain in the American Navy. But Captain McQueen was more than a warrior; he was a confidante of George Washington, serving as a courier between the general and Lafayette and the American representatives in France, Benjamin Franklin, and Thomas Jefferson. McQueen was a tall and handsome man of imposing presence; one of those personalities who are loved by women and admired by men—respected and trusted by the important and followed with awe by underlings. In a later era McQueen might have been a transcontinental railroad builder, a captain of industry, or a super-developer.

After the Revolutionary War, McQueen returned to South Carolina, but plantation life was dull. Prospects seemed brighter in Georgia, a developing state then enjoying a boom in land speculation. McQueen moved with his family to southern Georgia where he acquired a new plantation. His investment, together with speculations in real estate, put him deeply in debt. When creditors got hot on his coattail, threatening to put him in jail—yes, you could go to jail for debt in the 1700s—McQueen fled to Spanish Florida.

The history of Florida during the twenty years between 1763 and 1791, the year McQueen arrived, is a fascinating one. Britain had acquired Florida after trouncing France and Spain in the Seven Years War, ending in 1763. The Spanish were glad to trade Florida, which had been a headache for 250 years, to Britain in exchange for Havana, which the British had seized. While the Spanish had held to Florida only out of military necessity, making little effort to turn it into a productive colony, the British sought to make Florida pay its way by inviting colonists with promises of land grants. A large number came, particularly English loyalists during the Revolutionary War. They took up claims mainly along the Saint Johns, where fertile, well-drained soil was available, and because the river provided a means of transportation. Many of the settlers were successful, growing cotton, indigo, and producing sugar for export. But about the time the colonists had acclimated themselves to the new climate and had learned how to make the land profitably productive, Britain lost the war with its rebellious colonies, and decided, in 1783, that Florida was more of a.liability than an asset. With Florida situated between the United States and the Spanish possessions, and not worth the risk of war to defend, Britain simply gave it back to Spain in 1783.

During its previous occupation of Florida, Spain had refused to allow any foreigners to settle here. Being strictly a military operation, the Spanish wanted no spies or possible

"Fifth Columnists" to engage in intrigue. But after 1783 Florida was of much lesser military importance to Spain, and when the Spanish returned to Saint Augustine they adopted a liberal policy toward foreign settlers. Perhaps they saw how well the English and Scotch planters had done.

The policy proved a mistake. All the Spanish fears of spies and saboteurs during the earlier period were realized after 1790. Thomas Jefferson, Washington's secretary of state, suggested that 100,000 citizens take advantage of the Spanish offer. Wanting Florida for the United States, Jefferson suggested to President Washington that it might be possible to take Florida without firing a shot. No such numbers suggested by Jefferson came to Florida, but those that did made trouble enough. Among them was John Houston McIntosh, who took up a land grant on the Saint Johns at Ortega Point, now part of Jacksonville. The Spanish soon discovered that he was an agent of the United States and speeded him off to prison in Morro Castle in Havana, where he remained two years, until President Washington intervened to demand his release. Back to the Saint Johns he came, forgiven by the Spanish governor at Saint Augustine.

The irrepressible Captain McQueen arrived about the same time as McIntosh, taking up a grant of land on Fort George Island and establishing a cotton and indigo plantation. In 1792 McQueen built himself a modest home. Although no more than a cottage, it was well built of the best heart timber, and it still stands today.

From the correspondence between Captain McQueen and his wife, who remained in Georgia to manage the plantation there, we know that the Revolutionary War hero hoped to make enough money to pay off his debts and return home. But he soon was in St. Augustine, ingratiating himself with Governor Juan Quesada, and the next thing we hear is that "Don Juan" McQueen has the title of Commander of the Saint Johns, in charge of the Spanish navy on the river. But

McQueen was taken by the governor's charms, too, for he soon was converted to the Catholic faith. Wheeling and dealing between the Saint Johns and Saint Augustine, McQueen now maintained two homes and was engaged in a number of enterprises, including slave trading and lumbering, as well as farming. But more than a dozen years passed and Captain McQueen still had not paid off his debts.

After President Jefferson purchased Louisiana from France in 1803, shipping between the Gulf ports and the eastern seaboard increased enormously. It was all by sail, because no railroads connected the Mississippi Valley with the East, and all shipping had to pass through the Straits of Florida. A great many ships were driven onto the reefs by storms, or wound up there through poor navigation. Bahamans from New Providence, Eleuthera, and Abaco—many of whom were British loyalists who had left Florida after Britain returned it to Spain in 1783—preyed upon the wrecks. Small colonies of "wreckers" became established at Cape Florida, Indian Key, and Key West, on the edge of the Gulf Stream and the Florida Reef. These keys were owned by Spain, so the United States had no authority to intercede, while the Spanish governor lacked the navy to do anything.

This is where Don Juan McQueen enters the stage again. He obtained from the governor the exclusive license to do all the "wrecking" along the Florida coast. As a Spanish commander, McQueen was given authority to drive out the Bahamans and to establish his salvage operations—cutting the governor in on his profits, of course. Selling his plantation to John Houstoun McIntosh, McQueen made arrangements to outfit a score of sail. But in 1807, before he could get his new venture under way, Don Juan McQueen was stricken by a fatal heart attack. And instead of the governor going down to the docks to bid his commander farewell, he went to the cathedral, where was held one of the most colorful and extravagant funeral services in Saint Augustine's history.

After purchasing the McQueen plantation, McIntosh transferred his farming operations from Ortega Point to Fort George Island and moved into the McQueen house. Here, with encouragement from Washington, McIntosh continued his intrigue. His old friend, President Jefferson, was still anxious to add Florida to the United States, whose size he had doubled with the Louisiana Purchase. Although Jefferson ended his second term in 1809 without realizing his goal, his successor, James Madison, had been his secretary of state, and he shared Jefferson's ambition to annex Florida. But Madison's immediate aim was to acquire only a small area of northeast Florida, between the Saint Johns and Saint Marys rivers. This included what is today Nassau County and a portion of Duval County.

Madison wanted to acquire this bit of Florida because slave traders were using the port of Fernandina, at the mouth of the Saint Marys River almost within sight of Georgia. Congress during Jefferson's administration had passed an act outlawing any further importation of slaves into the United States. Illegal traffic in contraband human cargo became highly profitable, and Fernandina became the chief port of operations. The Spanish governor at Saint Augustine was powerless to stop the operations. By 1811 the trade in slaves had grown to scandalous proportions. Congress, in a secret vote, empowered Madison to annex the northeast Florida territory, along with Fernandina.

Meanwhile, McIntosh had been busy organizing local planters as "Patriots," pledging them to rise up with arms when called upon to help "win their freedom" from Spain. Madison sent his own agent, General George Mathews, another Revolutionary War veteran, to encourage and supervise his mission in Florida. Mathews arrived at the McIntosh cottage on Fort George Island in late 1811. Over a bottle of rum Mathews laid forth Madison's plans, for the planters of the Saint Johns to seize northeast Florida and turn it over to the United States. By the time the rum was finished off McIntosh was ready to declare war on the whole Spanish empire. He had not forgotten his two years in Morro Castle. Rounding up the planters, Mathews and McIntosh called a meeting on the Saint Marys River. The meeting developed into a convention and the election of John Houstoun McIntosh as president of the East Florida Republic. President Madison's limited objective was ignored. The planters, with the encouragement of Mathews and McIntosh, decided to seize Saint Augustine as well as Fernandina and declare all of the Florida peninsula an independent republic. Spain, engaged in war with Napoleon, would be unable to aid Florida, McIntosh's cabinet agreed.

Unaware that his limited objective had been expanded to include Saint Augustine, Madison sent Navy gunboats and a small Army unit to Fernandina while members of the Georgia militia, together with a following of ragtail Cracker frontiersmen, crossed into Florida-to join the Patriots. They marched on Fernandina, which, held by a Spanish officer and eight privates, was surrendered without a shot. The Patriots now turned toward Saint Augustine, which, with the help of U.S. gunboats, they sought to blockade. The Spanish retreated to Fort San Marcos and prepared to undergo a siege. But while the Patriots succeeded in closing the port, the Seminole Indians slipped past the night watches with food for the Spanish. The Seminoles were paying back the Americans for stealing their cattle.

In the meantime, reports of the Florida happenings reached Madison. He exploded, if that's what presidents do when they get the worst kind of news. By this time, in the early part of 1812, Madison was about to get involved in another war with Britain. Trouble with Spain he did not need. Apologizing to the Spanish, Madison laid the blame on General Mathews, who was retired from government service. Madison sent Governor Henry L. Mitchell of Georgia to call off the siege of Saint Augustine and to placate Spanish authorities. By this time the East Florida Republic was disintegrating. Madison already had recalled the Navy and the U.S. soldiers taking part in the rebellion, leaving only a nondescript army of planters, Georgia militia, and renegades. In the meantime, the Seminoles and runaway slaves had begun attacking the Patriots and laying waste to their plantations, scalping the non-Spanish whites they captured. Among the plantations attacked was that of Zephaniah Kingsley of Laurel Grove, now Orange Park. The attackers burned the houses, scalped three white workers, and carried off a number of slaves.

What was left of the army of the republic pulled back from Saint Augustine and hastened toward the Georgia border, along the way stealing everything that could be carried or driven, including cattle, horses, and slaves.

Did the Spanish hang McIntosh? Not at all. Patching up his differences with the Spanish, he returned to what had been for a time the "White House" of the East Florida Republic. But by this time McIntosh had squandered so much of his wealth in intrigue that he was broke. He borrowed large sums from Kingsley, wealthiest of the planters on the Saint Johns, and in 1817 he deeded the Fort George Plantation to him.

Kingsley was more than a colorful figure; he was certainly one of the most extraordinary personalities among the planters of the Saint Johns. He was a little man, just a bit over five feet in height, and he rode a tall white horse about his plantation, barking orders to his minions like a frontier edition of Napoleon. To disguise his small stature, he wore a colorful Mexican poncho and an enormous sombrero. But one also must imagine Kingsley as a man who had guts, wit, charm, and a convincing line of gab. He was able to stand up to the tough slave traders of the late eighteenth and early nineteenth centuries, able to deal with the savage African chiefs who sold their subjects to him. He was equal to the corruptness of the Spanish officials, the intrigue of the Saint Johns planters, and the United States.

A native of Scotland, Kingsley migrated to Charleston, South Carolina, as a youth and was there to welcome the British soldiers who took the city during the Revolutionary War. Almost nothing is known of Kingsley's life between 1780 and 1803 when he showed up in Florida to claim a grant of 3,000 acres on the Saint Johns at the present site of Orange Park. Today Orange Park's principal avenue bears his name, and so does one of north Florida's important lakes, near Starke. Kingsley maintained a home in Saint Augustine as well as on the Saint Johns, and owned a fleet of slaving ships. The banning of the importation of slaves by the United States in 1807 did not stop Kingsley. It had the effect of raising the price of slaves and meant more profit for Kingsley and the other slave smugglers who enjoyed the protection of the Spanish government in Florida.

Kingsley, however, had unique ideas about slavery—"advanced" ideas, they were called at the time. In a treatise he wrote on slave management and training, Kingsley expressed the opinion that some men were better off under bondage than free, but he advocated humane treatment and proposed that slaves could be trained to do tasks requiring greater skill than merely working in fields or doing domestic jobs. To prove his theory, Kingsley trained slaves as carpenters and masons, selling them for twice the price he could get for an ordinary field hand.

Kingsley traveled to Africa himself, where he dealt personally with the strong slave-capturing chiefs. In Senegal he met Princess Anna Madgegine Jai, daughter of an important chief, and took a fancy for her. Winning her hand and her father's consent, Kingsley married the princess in elaborate tribal rites. Returning to Florida, Kingsley put her over his slaves. Recognizing her as a royal person, the slaves addressed her as "Ma'am Anna" and observed the customary obsequites demanded by an African princess. Ma'am Anna ran the plantation while her husband was away on trips. But Princess Anna was only Kingsley's chief wife. While he never had a white wife, Kingsley lived with several of his young slave women, as he indicates in his unique will, which mentions his mulatto offspring. One of his wives, Musilna McGundo, and her daughter by him, Fatima, were given a life tenancy in "Tabby House," the ruins of which still stand alongside the shell road leading to the Kingsley house on Fort George Island.

After the Seminoles burned his plantation houses in 1812, Kingsley became disenchanted with Orange Park. Taking over the McIntosh plantation in 1817, he moved to Fort George Island where he built a two-story house facing Fort George Sound, some sixty feet from the cottage McQueen had built in 1792. The two houses were connected by a covered veranda. Atop the new house Kingsley had a "captain's walk," or mirador, built so that he could observe his ships as they came up Fort George Sound on an incoming tide. The McQueen house became known as the Ma'am Anna house, because his chief wife lived there. Kingsley built a string of tabby quarters—of oyster shell and limestone construction— for his slaves. The ruins of these quarters still stand, although only the walls and the chimneys survive.

Just how Kingsley had his empire organized we don't know. He avoided maintaining records, especially a journal, probably because of possible incrimination. Although he managed to maintain cordial relations with the Spanish governor, he was in bad graces with the United States because of his slave smuggling operations. However, after the destruction of his plantation houses during the East Florida Republic fiasco, Kingsley sued the United States and collected $73,000 in damages. He appears to have given up the illegal slave trade after 1817 when President Monroe sent the Navy to Fernandina to put a stop to the smuggling. And in 1821, when Florida was transferred to the United States by Spain, Kingsley was appointed one of thirteen members of a council created to govern the new territory. President Monroe described him as one of the "most fit and discreet persons in the territory."

Before his death in 1843, Kingsley sent Princess Ma'am Anna Madgegine Jai Kingsley and her children by him to Haiti where he owned a plantation, which he presumably gave to her. Nothing is known today of Kingsley's offspring.

A sister of Kingsley, Isabella, and her husband, George Gibbs, moved onto the Kingsley plantation in 1821, and presumably Gibbs took over some part of the management. A son, Kingsley Beatty Gibbs, grew up on the plantation and took over the operation after his Uncle Zephaniah's death in New York. Nephew Gibbs lived in the Kingsley house until 1869, after which it was sold to the John F. Rollins family, which made some changes but kept the house in good repair during half a century of occupancy. The state of Florida acquired the Kingsley and McQueen houses in 1955, together with the slave quarters and "Tabby House." Although the Kingsley house has been furnished with furniture of the early 1800s, most of the furniture which Kingsley owned has disappeared. As you are guided through the house today, you are shown where Kingsley had his bed and his desk, and the guide may point to a "jail" he maintained in the attic for "unruly slaves." But it must have been "mildly" unruly slaves that were kept here, for the jail doesn't appear to be strong enough to hold anyone determined to get out. However, in the basement is an old wooden stock, used in Kingsley's time for securing the legs of slaves, either as a means of punishment or to prevent escape. There is no evidence the stock belonged to Kingsley.

While I was visiting the Kingsley house a group of three young blacks appeared and asked to see the stock. They asked to see nothing else; they apparently had no interest in the house. Taken to the basement, they looked at the stock in silence. Finally one of them moaned. Then the three turned and departed.

THREE

A Stroll Through History

If you are a person who finds the reading of history dull; if you want to be shown where history happened—shown some relic that helps to make history come to life—well, Saint Augustine is that kind of city. Once you have penetrated the gaudy signs promoting a multitude of attractions, designed to get their share of the tourist dollar; once you have gained entry into the old city—the Plaza, St. George Street, Charlotte Street, or Fort San Carlos—you can forget the twentieth century, and, for a time, at least, return to the eighteenth, even the seventeenth century.

Fort San Marcos—Castillo de San Marcos National Monument—one of the finest relics of its kind in the Americas, was built between 1672 and 1696. When you cross the drawbridge that spans the water-filled moat and enter the sally port you are walking into history that you can feel and touch, even smell in the dank guard rooms. Here on the walls are drawings of sailing ships, traced in the stone-hard coquina stone by some homesick member of the guard perhaps two centuries ago. Little imagination is needed to know what that soldier was thinking; he wanted to go home, back to Spain where there was good bread, olive oil, and wine, none of which could be produced in Florida.

This old fort is really a castle, as the name "castillo" implies. By the time work on San Marcos was begun, they had stopped building castles with great towers and high battlements, like those popular in the Middle Ages. Those high walls were too easily knocked down by artillery fire. Castillo de San Marcos was built low, with twelve-foot-thick walls that could resist the impact of exploding cannon balls, and large enough for the population of the Saint Augustine colony to retreat and live during a siege. Several of the rooms within the coquina walls have been restored, enabling you to see where the Spanish stored food so that 2,000 troops and civilians could live for weeks while the fort was under attack. And Castillo de San Marcos was under attack several times, but never taken. Governor James Moore of South Carolina burned the city in 1702 but failed to take the fort. Governor James Oglethorpe failed in two tries, in 1740 and 1743. So did the forces of the East Florida Republic under the leadership of President John Houstoun McIntosh, even though they had the assistance of United States troops and gunboats.

Work on San Marcos was begun in 1672, after an English pirate, John Davis, had sacked the town in 1668. Spanish craftsmen, English prisoners of war, Indian slaves, and black slaves—the first black slaves to be used in North America—worked for twenty-four years to complete the four bastions, moat, and outer defenses. But as late as 1756 improvements were being made; and the English added a second floor of rooms about the courtyard during their occupation of Florida between 1763 and 1783.

Spain established Saint Augustine in 1565 to clinch its claim to Florida after French Hugenots built Fort Caroline on the Saint Johns River, some six miles from its mouth, in 1564. The Spanish built a fort of pine logs at Saint Augustine—a stockade around a group of houses—and called it San Juan de Piños. Saint John was a small help, however, when Sir Francis Drake attacked Saint Augustine twenty-one years later with his motley cutthroats. Turning cannon on the pine pole fort, Drake breached the walls and slew most of the frightened defenders. Sir Francis departed with Saint Augustine's bronze cannon and some $20,000 worth of silver, which the colonists probably had retrieved from the wreck of a Spanish treasure ship on a Florida beach.

The survivors, relieved by the addition of troops and supplies from Havana, rebuilt Fort San Juan de Piños, while the Spanish governor sought in vain for money, technicians, and black slaves to build a stronger fort. Coquina had been discovered in great abundance on nearby Anastasia Island, across Matanzas River from Saint Augustine. But despite the settlement by the British of Jamestown in 1607 and Plymouth in 1620, the Spanish did nothing to improve the defenses of Saint Augustine until after a visit by Pirate John Davis in 1668. The settlement of Charleston by English colonists in 1670 may have given some impetus to a decision by the Spanish to hasten the building of Fort San Marcos.

The fort sits on what was once an ancient Indian midden, on Matanzas River. Outside the walls, the midden, now covered with lawn grass, rolls away on three sides, giving the defenders a clear view and command of all approaches—the Inlet, Matanzas River, and the land. The National Park Service has planted cabbage palms and other trees about the fort, adding to a group of cedars planted near the entrance possibly a century ago. When San Marcos was Spain's sole means of defending Florida from seizure by the English colonists and the freebooters plundering the Atlantic, no trees or

growth of any kind that might give an enemy any protection
were permitted within a cannon shot of the fort. But the
plantings, carefully done by Park Service landscape designers,
have relieved the sprawling fort and the spacious grounds
about it of their starkness. The live oaks, the gnarled old
cedars, and the more recently planted cabbage palms—
century-old specimens brought in from the nearby woods—
give the seventeenth-century relic a charm that is unsurpassed
in Florida. My wife and I have spent many hours of enjoyment, strolling through the grounds outside the walls, viewing
the bastions, shaped like immense arrowheads, from every
direction. Many views of the fort are beautiful, even picturesque, putting one in the contemplative mood that helps one
to enjoy this relic of man's ingenuity, energy, and determi-
nation to survive. The National Park Service has made Castillo de San Marcos a monument that breathes the colorful
history of Saint Augustine, with all the romance of centuries
behind it, together with the cruelties and the tragedies that
are part of both victory and defeat.

San Marcos has been more than a fort; it has served also as
a prison. The English, during their twenty-year possession of
Florida, kept colonial prisoners of the Revolutionary War
here. Among them were three signers of the Declaration of
Independence, Edward Rutledge, Thomas Heyward, and
Arthur Middleton, captured when the British seized Charleston. After Spain ceded Florida to the United States in 1821,
Castillo de San Marcos became Fort Marion, in honor of
Francis Marion, Revolutionary War hero whom the British
nicknamed "The Fox." Fort Marion became an Indian prison
after the beginning of the 1835-42 Seminole War. Osceola
was the most famous of its prisoners. He was transferred to
prison in Charleston where he died. But Chief Coacoochee, or
Wildcat, escaped from the prison in 1837 and rejoined his
people in their fight against U.S. troops. A tour of the fort
takes you through the cell from which Wildcat escaped. Wild-

cat starved himself until he could slip through a narrow window. The fort served again as an Indian prison in the 1880s when Geronimo's Apaches were on the warpath in the West. It was last used by the military during the Spanish-American War, when the Army confined court-martialed troops here.

For a quarter century the fort was neglected. Then in 1924 President Coolidge signed a proclamation declaring it a national monument. More than a million dollars has been spent by the National Park Service in preservation and restoration. The fort is now Florida's most popular historic relic.

San Marcos is, of course, one of countless relics of old Saint Augustine that hold attraction to visitors. Catholics have a special interest in the city, because it was here that the first Spanish mission, Nombre de Dios, was established in North America. Here the Shrine of Our Lady of La Leche is maintained in a setting that Catholics refer to as America's "most sacred acre."

The Catholic Church has spent more than two million dollars since 1965 in a building and restoration program to mark the four-hundredth anniversary of Catholicism in North America. Much of the work has been more than restoration; it has been a glorification of the church as much as a bow to history, such as the erection of a 200-foot stainless steel cross which dominates the view north of San Marcos. The Cathedral, facing the Plaza, has been almost completely rebuilt behind a two-century-old facade. More striking in architecture, although of less historic interest, is Flagler Memorial (Presbyterian) Church. Designed in Venetian Renaissance style, the church's huge copper dome rises 129 feet. Flagler built the church in 1890 in memory of his daughter, Jenny Louise, who died in 1889 at the age of 34. Like the Cathedral, the Flagler Memorial Church is open to the public. Flagler was buried here after his death at Palm Beach in 1913.

You need two or three days to see Saint Augustine, to become familiar with the old city and its history, and have

time to stroll the streets and revisit sites of special interest. I like particularly the walk from the fort, through the City Gate at the entrance to St. George Street, and the four-block walk south on St. George Street to the Plaza. I find many of the restored buildings of less interest inside than the stroll itself, beneath balconied windows, past doorways like you see in Latin America and Spain.

My favorite of the privately owned attractions in Saint Augustine is the Oldest House, owned and operated by the Saint Augustine Historical Society. Its furnishings are authentic, in that they belong to the colonial era, and the interior and gardens have been done so well that the Oldest House might be considered almost a work of art. Prior to its purchase in 1918 by the historical society, it had been promoted as the "Oldest House in the United States." But anyone acquainted with the history of Saint Augustine knows that no structure in the city except the fort itself dates back farther than 1702, when Governor Moore of South Carolina set fire to all the houses after a twenty-seven-day siege of the fort proved unsuccessful. After a thorough historical and archaeological study of the house was made the name was shortened to "Oldest House." With a story steeped in the history of Saint Augustine back to the seventeen-hundreds, the Oldest House became second only to Fort San Carlos as an attraction. Guides emphasize the story of the people who resided here during the Spanish and English occupations and how they lived.

Much of the rustic atmosphere of Saint Augustine that Henry M. Flagler must have admired while on his honeymoon here during the winter of 1883-84 has disappeared. Saint Augustine was then a sleepy town which came to life with enthusiasm and lively color during festive occasions. No gaudy signs called attention to its attractions. Despite its quietness, Flagler liked Saint Augustine so well that he returned the following year, and it was on this visit that he witnessed a festival celebrating the landing of Ponce de León in 1513. Dressed in costumes of the sixteenth century, Saint Augustinians, many of whom could trace their ancestors to Spanish times, put on a lively spectacle that captivated Flagler, who was at that time secretly buying property in Saint Augustine and planning to build a luxury hotel. Flagler decided not only to name his hotel after Ponce de León but to build it in the Spanish Renaissance style of the early sixteenth century.

Although it long ago outlived its usefulness as a hotel and now serves as the home of a girls' college, the Ponce de Leon survives as the most striking example of nineteenth-century hotel architecture in Florida. The Tampa Hotel, opened in 1891 by Henry Plant, deserves the title of most bizarre hotel structure in the state, but for the extravagance of its design— for the bravado of its towers and emphasis on luxury—no other hotel ever built in Florida can be compared with the Ponce de Leon. Its poured concrete walls are four feet thick. During the arduous pouring in 1886 and 1887 song leaders were paid to keep the 1,200 construction workers happy. Like Castillo de San Marcos, the Ponce de Leon is a monument to labor, as well as to the genius of its architects, Thomas Hastings and John M. Carrere, of New York. Hastings and Carrere also designed the beautiful Flagler Memorial Church in Saint Augustine, as well as Whitehall, the mansion Flagler built in Palm Beach for his third wife, the lovely Mary Lily Kenan. Whitehall is today maintained as a museum, a relic of a period when industrialists like Flagler and Rockefeller would amass immense fortunes and build their own private empires.

In 1967 I journeyed up to Saint Augustine to do an article for *The Miami Herald* on the scheduled closing of the Ponce de León as a hotel and plans for its conversion into Flagler College for girls. I was shown about the hotel by its manager, who introduced me to several of the elderly guests.

"For many guests it will be a sad ending," I wrote in an article which the editor entitled "The Passing of a Palace." "Many are about as old as the hotel, and they have been spending a part of each winter here for several years. There's something about the hotel that has made it attractive to older people. Possibly it's the atmosphere of bygone days when bustled ladies in yards of silk added luster to the magnificent building.

"The Ponce de Leon was Flagler's first project in Florida. It was the beginning of a career in hotel and railway building that was to end with the completion of the Overseas Railway to Key West in 1912, a year before the millionaire oilman's death. Although the Ponce de Leon made architectural history in the United States, its life as a watering spot for wealthy sun-seekers was short. For by 1894, just six years after its opening, Flagler had extended his Florida East Coast Railway to Palm Beach, to another magnificent tourist hotel, the Royal Poinciana. And two years later the railroad reached Miami and Flagler's Royal Palm Hotel.

"So, while the Ponce de Leon held its position as an architectural delight, the richly jeweled ladies and their cigar-smoking escorts had moved southward. Now in its final days you can rent a room at the Ponce for less than a room costs in the better motels about town. But for atmosphere, you couldn't beat the Ponce anywhere else in America or Europe. Except for one thing: you have the feeling of being in an old folks' home. Without the youth of former years, the atmosphere seems dismal, even with the fine tinted glass windows and the celebrated wall and ceiling paintings done by George W. Maynard, whose murals also decorate the Library of Congress.

"The wonderful thing about the conversion of the Ponce de Leon into a college is that its art and architecture will be preserved. . . . Presumably the fine old bar will become a college canteen; but the lively girls who inhabit the building will

always have a poem by Shenstone, set in the tile near the
dining room entrance, to remind them that Flagler College
was once a hotel:

> "Who'er has travel'd life's dull round
> Where'er his stages may have been
> May sigh to think he still has found
> The warmest welcome at an Inn."

I was shown a suite of rooms where a Vanderbilt might
have slept in 1889, paying $100 a day, and invited by the
manager to stay and "get the feel" of the Ponce de Leon
before attempting to write my story. But I declined. Somehow I preferred my $15 room at Howard Johnson's. There
was something utterly lonely and forbidding about the Ponce
de Leon suite. Nor did I like the idea of being the only
"young" person staying at the hotel. Although at that time I
was in my late fifties, still most of the guests appeared to be
in their seventies or beyond—mostly elderly women whose
husbands had passed on. But I did return that evening for a
last opportunity to dine in the luxurious dining room and for
another look at the beautiful tile and the magnificent walls
and ceilings done by outstanding artists of the nineteenth
century. As I studied the Spanish proverbs on the walls and
ceilings, I remembered being told that the young women at-
tending Flagler College would have an opportunity to major
in Spanish with Spanish history and Spanish culture as prime
subjects. How appropriate, I thought, and wondered if being
able to translate the proverbs, set in tile on the walls, like
"Quien mas sabe mas calla" (A still tongue makes a wise
head) would be a prerequisite for graduation. This, I concluded, would be a sobering thought for 400 young females.

FOUR

The Ormond Still Lives

In 1887 when Henry M. Flagler was completing his luxurious Ponce de Leon Hotel in Saint Augustine, fifty miles south another hotel was going up. Although a wooden structure costing a fraction of the Ponce de Leon, the Ormond Hotel was to become one of the best-known resort hotels in the world. And it stands today, the largest wooden structure in Florida and among the largest in the world.

The Ormond is still in operation, but its guests are no longer nineteenth-century capitalists and their families; they are elderly residents, content to live with the ghosts of the Astors, Goulds, Rockefellers, and Vanderbilts—enjoying the same comforts if not the same affluence.

Sprawling along the east side of the quiet Halifax River, the white structure rises, hospitallike, from a grove of cabbage palms. A factory-size smokestack adds to the hospital image.

Although the conglomerate of buildings looks immense, you cannot appreciate the size until you have strolled the length of one of the porches, or until you have read the statistics—eleven miles of porches and breezeways, together with 350 bedrooms, many with parlors. And if this is not enough to give you a picture, add the lobby, the size of a baseball diamond; a dining room seating more than 300; and a kitchen the size of a small auditorium. The Ormond had more than 400 rooms before its south wing was trimmed back for the widening of Granada Avenue, which extends through the town from the ocean across the river.

On the day I visited the Ormond some 175 elderly residents were living there the year round, and I was told that in the fall this number was doubled as winter guests arrived. All those I saw were old and gray, many of them marked by the stresses of the years they had lived. A check of ages revealed that residents were between sixty and ninety-four.

It was in the Ormond's early years that life was so plush; when a man wore a tuxedo to dinner, with his woman, dressed in silk and wearing her jewels, clinging to his arm as they entered the dining room where a hundred superbly trained European waiters provided faultless service. A uniformed butler announced mealtimes, including breakfast at 9:00 A.M. for early risers. Although few entered the surf during the winter, there were many things to do: play golf, hunt, fish, take trips on the Halifax River, or take a launch up the Tomaka River, one of the primatively beautiful streams in Florida, for a picnic lunch at a pavilion built for guests. After the turn of the century there were the demonstrations and trials of "horseless carriages," as the nation entered the automobile age, and guests flocked to the Ormond beach to watch the mechanical contraptions chug over the surface of the hard sand.

The Ormond Hotel was then open from January 1 to Easter. Prices were high, but so popular did the hotel become

that several additions were made in succeeding years. The
wealthy came in their luxurious private railway cars. A spur
railroad track spanned the Halifax River, and the cars were
pushed across by small steam engines, their cabbage-shaped
stacks belching tar-laden black smoke from the fat pine used
to heat their boilers. After the passengers left the cars, with
wardrobe trunks and massive suitcases, together with valets
and maids, the cars were drawn away and parked on side
tracks to wait until their owners were ready to move on
down to Palm Beach for gambling at Bradley's Casino, or to
Miami for the fishing in Biscayne Bay.

But when the Ormond opened on January 1, 1888, the
railroad went no farther than Daytona, a port on the Halifax
River a few miles south of Ormond. The builders of the
Ormond, James D. Price of Kentucky and John Anderson of
Maine, must have been entrepreneurs of unusual vision. They
had come to Ormond in the mid-1870s. When they began
talking about building a hotel in the wilderness between the
Halifax River and the Atlantic Ocean their friends thought
they had gone off their rockers. The railroad was still fifty
miles away. There was no bridge across the Halifax. And
neither Price nor Anderson had any money. In 1886, however, they discussed their plans with S. V. White, wealthy
Wall Street operator, who had discovered the Ormond-
Daytona area, together with the picturesque Halifax River
and the "widest ocean beach in the world." White not only
agreed to back Price and Anderson, but he built a railroad
from East Palatka to Ormond and Daytona, and he spanned
the Halifax with a bridge so wealthy guests could be delivered
to the hotel in their private railway cars.

Meanwhile, Henry M. Flagler had watched the building of
the Ormond with some uneasiness, because he feared it might
become a competitor to his Ponce de Leon. But as it turned
out, he need not have had any concern, because the owners
of the Ormond, unwise in the operation of a resort situated

at the end of "nowhere," got very few guests during their first two seasons. Nor did White's railroad pay off. So in 1890 the wealthy Flagler bought both hotel and railroad. The first thing he did was to paint the hotel "Flagler yellow," a color he was to use on his train stations and section bosses' houses from one end of the Florida East Coast Railway to the other. Next, he added a south wing to the Ormond, and in 1904 he added a west wing.

In the early 1900s the Ormond beach became the world's best-known automobile testing ground. Barney Oldfield, Ralph De Palma, and William K. Vanderbilt, Jr., established world speed records here and consistently broke them. If you were anything in the automobile world in 1903 you could be seen in the lobby of the Ormond Hotel. The famous Ormond Garage, where the drivers worked on their cars, still stands facing Granada Avenue and backing up to the eighteen-hole golf course Flagler built in the early 1890s. Henry Ford came in the winter of 1904, but, being too poor to stay at the expensive Ormond, slept in the flivver he had brought down to demonstrate.

Among the Ormond's early visitors was Flagler's partner in the Standard Oil Company, John D. Rockefeller. But the oil magnate, by then described as the world's richest man, wanted more privacy than a suite of rooms provided. He rented the entire second floor of the west wing, and here he lived each winter until 1917 when he bought the Casements, a large house across Granada Avenue from the hotel. The wing where Rockefeller and his family stayed became known as the "Rockefeller Wing," while the south wing became the "Flagler Wing." Both names persist. Rockefeller brought the Ormond worldwide publicity. He played almost daily on the Ormond's golf course, where he was frequently photographed with celebrities, including, in the 1920s and 1930s, such personalities as the Prince of Wales (the late Duke of Windsor) and Will Rogers. Photographers sought to catch Rockefeller giving his famous dime tip, which in his later years he gave even to celebrities after an afternoon on the golf links. Everyone sought a new "Rockefeller dime" as a souvenir. But the most widely used photograph showed Will Rogers giving Rockefeller a dime—a gimmick that paid off for the publicity agent who thought up the idea.

After Rockefeller's death at the Casements in 1937 the Ormond rapidly declined in popularity. It was no longer paying its way in 1949 when the Flagler System sold the hotel, together with the golf course and other valuable adjoining properties. For a time the Ormond became a hotel management school, but the project proved unsuccessful and the owner, Robert Woodward, sold off the golf course separately and put the hotel up for sale—for $175,000.

At Sanford, fifty miles away, the Reverend C. A. Maddy heard that the Ormond was for sale. He later would declare that the turn of events was an act of God. Maddy was at that time looking for a new home to house 100 retired preachers, missionaries, and other religiously congenial people who lived in the barracks of a World War II Air Force base at Sanford. The Korean War was in progress and the government had decided to reactivate the base. Maddy was given short notice to move his "family" out. But Maddy had no money. He had been forced to sell a piano in order to buy food for his group. Second, he had no idea of where to go even if he had money. Only one thing was left for a preacher to do: pray. He did—all day.

That night Maddy had a dream—or was it a vision? A group of sprawling white buildings with green shutters appeared before his eyes. In the foreground was a quiet, dark river, while in the distance ocean swells rolled in, broke over a bar, then rushed upon a broad, gray beach where they spent themselves in white foam. This familiar scene galvanized the waking preacher. It was none other than the Ormond Hotel, the Flagler yellow having been repainted white. Maddy mut-

tered a prayer of thanks to the Lord as he shaved. He wasted
no time in getting started toward Ormond.

Broke but sure the Lord would provide, Maddy called upon
Woodward. He wanted to buy the hotel but admitted he had
no money. Woodward assured him that terms could be arranged. But while the Lord may have accompanied him to
Ormond, he backed into the shadows as the two men bargained. The preacher began asking what went with the hotel,
and the seller frequently found it convenient to say:

"No, that's not part of the deal; if you want that it will
cost you extra."

By the time the two men got down to signing a contract,
the naive man of God had talked the price up $25,000. But
at least Maddy had a home for his big family, which he
immediately began moving from Sanford. The name of the
hotel he changed to Fellowship Center. Moreover, Maddy had
not paid a cent down.

Finding himself in possession of a hotel with 400 rooms
but with only 100 occupants, Maddy began searching his
mind and praying to God for ideas. The idea came, in a
vision, of course, and he could claim it the biggest single idea
of a lifetime. It was a new plan for taking care of the aged.
He would sell them lifetime-care contracts. Maddy appears to
have had no special formula. A man of God, he needed only
the idea; God would provide the details. A confident, easy,
and fluid talker, he found it not difficult to learn after a few
minutes of conversation with a prospect how much his life's
savings amounted to. If he had saved $4,000, then Maddy
offered him a contract providing lifetime care for him and his
wife, plus a part of the social security they received. If the
savings totaled $6,000, that was the price, and so on.

One who knew Maddy well and was intimately acquainted
with his dealings described the preacher as a person who had
reached the level of "sinless perfection" in his religious pur-
suits. He was above questioning about right or wrong. What-

ever he decided to do had to be right because God was at his elbow to guide him and would let him do nothing that was not right. And so successful was his sale of lifetime-care contracts that he soon filled the Ormond. Money was rolling in. Never had Maddy seen so much. He had found a gold mine. And, now, having attributed the idea to God, he concluded that his boundless success meant that the Lord wanted him to open additional centers so that he could take care of a greater number of elderly people. The first place to catch his envious eye was the Casements, the former home of John D. Rockefeller. Then he began purchasing large homes and run-down hotels in other cities. Countless inquiries were coming in daily from elderly persons who had heard of the Maddy plan. In interviews he quickly sized up the prospects who had money and had little trouble in getting them to turn over their life's savings to him. With a growing business that appeared to be a highly profitable one, Maddy found it convenient to set up a corporation. On the board he put a number of well-to-do persons who had contributed to his "humanitarian program" for caring for the aged. They understood that their position on the board was more or less honorary and they did not bother to raise any questions about Maddy's operations.

In the meantime, a wealthy retired candy manufacturer of Tarpon Springs, Edgar H. Cook, became interested in Maddy's program. Cook, in his nineties, sold his home and moved into Maddy's Fellowship Center at Ormond. A person of fervent religious beliefs. Cook was much impressed by Maddy's desire to do good for his fellow man. After conferring with Maddy, he decided to put $150,000 into the preacher's enterprise. Maddy then made a mistake. He put Cook on the board of directors. With nothing better to do, the aged man began to take an interest in the financial structure of the enterprise. He soon discovered that the picture given him by Maddy was altogether exaggerated. Moreover, the preacher was so naive about business matters that he could not even read a financial report. To Maddy these were mundane things for clerks to worry about. Nor did the discovery by Cook that the enterprise was on the verge of bankruptcy concern Maddy. When he sought to call the preacher's hand, Maddy brushed aside his concerns with the reminder that the Lord would take care, "as He, in His wisdom, always has."

Although in his nineties, Cook possessed his mental faculties. Moreover, he had behind him a lifetime of experience in a highly competitive business. Employing an attorney, Cook filed a suit to force the Fellowship Center into receivership and kick Maddy out. Then, with the help of a local businessman, Cook formed the New Ormond Hotel Corporation. The discovery of his prodigious failure was an immense shock to Maddy. The preacher returned to central Florida, where he sought to reestablish the reputation of his care program, but he died of a heart attack in the early 1960s. Cook, too, has gone to his Maker, but the corporation he organized is still intact, although operated in a much different way from the lifetime-care deal Maddy had offered. Guests at the Ormond simply pay on a monthly basis for lodging and meals.

Those I talked with during a visit to the Ormond, to do a story on its present operation for *The Miami Herald,* appeared to be happy enough with their situation. They liked the idea of living in a hotel that once was a famous tourist resort, frequented by the rich and affluent. The rooms are comfortable in the winter because the hotel is steam-heated, but there is no air conditioning to cool the rooms during the long hot summers. Nearly all the guests I talked to appeared to have enough income to live comfortably almost anywhere if costs were moderate. The only really indigent people I found living in the Ormond were the survivors of the Reverend Maddy's lifetime-care program. The new corporation, which inherited these persons who had handed their life savings to Maddy, will be given their meals and lodging for the rest of their lives, I was told.

At the invitation of the management, my wife and I ate a dinner in the spacious dining room. What impressed us most was the way the guests dressed for dinner. Although the former diners in this spacious room may have had finer clothes, they could not have been more proud than the modern gentlemen and ladies. Some even paused for a moment at the entrance, as if waiting for a tuxedo-clad maitre d' to seat them. Then they moved on to the buffet where they served themselves, army style, stew meat, mashed potatoes, peas, and cabbage slaw. Although the food was only fair, it was substantial, and guests could eat all they wanted, including Jello for dessert.

Among the guests I talked with were Mr. and Mr. Joseph LeMaire of New York. They invited me to see their suite of rooms—a large living room, bedroom, and bath—where they lived the year round. LeMaire had been a violinist with the Metropolitan Opera for thirty years before retiring. The hotel manager had introduced me to LeMaire because the musician had played with the Ormond Hotel orchestra during the winters of 1909 and 1910.

"I'll bet he could tell you a lot about what the Ormond was like in those days," said the manager.

But LeMaire could recall nothing, except the "wonderful two winters," which did "get cold" at times. He also remembered how warm and pleasant it was in the hotel and how cold the unheated quarters were where the musicians lived.

"We had ice in our water bucket one night—and it was inside the house," said LeMaire.

But not a thing could he remember about the guests, who they were, how they dressed, or what they did. Except that they "danced in the evenings after dinner and acted exactly like the guests I've played for in other hotels," he said.

"I guess I was just thinking about home," he added.

It was time to leave when LeMaire, urged by his wife, did recall an event that happened during the winter of 1910 while he was playing at the Ormond. His wife gave birth to a son, which he did not see until he returned home.

"We named him Ormond," said LeMaire.

"Ormond lives at Long Island," added Mrs. LeMaire.

FIVE

Those Rowdy Minorcans

✐

More than two centuries have passed since 1,255 Mediterranean colonists, hopeful of finding a better way of life, landed on the palm-fringed Mosquito Lagoon sixty-five miles south of Saint Augustine. Except for an irrigation ditch or two and the stone foundation of a house, nothing remains to prove that the colonists were here except the name of the community, New Smyrna. But although the colony was a spectacular failure, the offspring of the survivors have contributed a colorful chapter in the history of the New World. Among them have been bankers, businessmen, fishermen, outstanding men of letters, political leaders, priests, and soldiers, as well as countless unique and unforgettable characters.

Stephen Vincent Benét, whose ancestors came with the Minorcan colony—as the settlers became known—was

awarded the Pulitzer prize in 1929 for his book-length poem, *John Brown's Body*. Benét's brother, William Rose Benét, was a founder of the *Saturday Review of Literature*. The father of the Benét brothers was a general in the United States Army, while their grandfather, Pedro Benét, one of Saint Augustine's most colorful personalities, was known as the "King of the Minorcans." He was a political leader during the Civil War.

A relative, Charles (Bossy) Benet—he pronounced his name to rhyme with Bennet as many other Benets now do—was Saint Augustine's marshal for several years after the turn of the century. Bossy Benet was a handsome man of medium build, with silvery hair and a dyed mustache that matched his intense black eyes. Old-timers remember when Bossy whipped out his revolver at a council meeting and shot a councilman. Bossy had asked the council to buy new uniforms for the police force. Councilman John Papino, another Minorcan, got up to speak against the motion. Bossy ordered him to sit down and keep quiet. The offended councilman shook his fist in Bossy's face and informed him he had no right to speak to an elected official like that. Whereupon Bossy drew his revolver and shot the councilman in the face. The councilman survived and so did Bossy.

A priest who attempted to build a balcony onto his quarters, extending it over the edge of a street in violation of a city ordinance, was quick to experience Bossy's wrath. The priest made the mistake of persisting in the construction after Bossy ordered him to stop and tear down what he already had built. Whereupon Bossy obtained a saw and sawed off the balcony, dumping the priest and his unfinished balcony into the street.

No Minorcan in recent years received so much publicity as Holsted (Hoss) Manucy did in 1964 when he told the nation through the various press associations that there would be no integration of blacks and whites in Saint Augustine. Two hundred and twenty pounds of brawn, and wearing a cowboy hat and string tie, the hot-headed Manucy emerged for a week as the ideal of the Florida redneck. He took on Martin Luther King, the governor of Florida, and the citizens of Saint Augustine who were agreeable to see the black people obtain their civil rights. A week of violence and head-skinning followed after King sought to help the frustrated blacks integrate the restaurants, swimming pools, and beaches. Seeing that Saint Augustine's police and sheriff's deputies were unable to keep order, Governor Farris Bryant sent in the Florida Highway Patrol—and it was now the rednecks whose heads got skinned. The city was seized from the firebrands and returned to the citizens of Saint Augustine. Hoss Manucy, summoned by a federal grand jury, took the fifth admendment. He soon returned to the oblivion which his fellow Minorcans thought he deserved.

Minorcans have played major roles in Saint Augustine, for good or for bad, ever since they settled there in 1777. For more than a century, from the time Spain ceded Florida to the United States in 1821 until just before World War II, Saint Augustine was dominated by the former New Smyrna colonists. Sticking together at the polls, the Minorcans were able to capture the important political posts. But otherwise they disagreed among themselves violently. Strongly individualistic, hot-tempered, and aggressive, they continually fought one another, giving Saint Augustine one of the most unstable city governments in Florida. Not until recent years, after the Minorcan population was diluted by newcomers who were often quick to marry the attractive, dark-eyed women, has Saint Augustine had a stable government.

But to get the full flavor of the Minorcans' history, you must return to 1768 when a Scotch physician, Dr. Andrew Turnbull, with the help of wealthy Englishmen, sought to establish a lucrative farm colony in Florida. Only five years before, England had acquired Florida from Spain in exchange

for Havana, which British troops had captured during the
Seven Years' war. British subjects were invited to colonize
Florida and a land boom followed. Dr. Turnbull contracted
the land fever and managed to infect several wealthy Lon-
doners with it. Selling his dream of a huge plantation to
produce cotton, indigo, sugar, and silk, Turnbull obtained a
grant in 1766 of 60,000 acres, which later grew to more than
100,000 acres. For colonists, Turnbull decided on inhabitants
of the Mediterranean because they were accustomed to a
warm climate, bred to the culture of the grape and the olive
which the physician hoped to grow in Florida. He was thinking particularly of the Greeks of the Levant, whom he had
become acquainted with during several years of government
service and where he had married the beautiful daughter of a
wealthy merchant. He thought of the Greeks as sober, indus-
trious, and even-tempered.

The site Turnbull selected for his settlement was on the
west side of the Mosquito Lagoon, five miles south of Ponce
de León Inlet. In 1767 he ordered the property surveyed and,
with funds provided by his backers, ordered a ship load of
black slaves from Africa—500 of them—to begin clearing the
land in advance of the arrival of the colonists. Then he set
out to the Mediterranean to pick up an equal number of
colonists. But only 200 Greeks would sign up, despite their
miserable poverty, and Turnbull sailed to Corsica. Here the
most he could get were 110 Italian men. At Minorca, in the
Balearic Islands, he found hundreds, even thousands, ready to
sign up. A famine was in progress, due to crop failures, and
the Minorcans were ready to sign a contract to go anywhere
in exchange for food.

When Turnbull's fleet of eight ships departed from Gibraltar on April 17, 1768, on board were 1,403 colonists, 900
more than he had planned to take. More than 150 died during the voyage, but there were a number of births. Upon
arriving in Minorca a year before departure, nearly half the

Corsican men married Minorcan women, and many of the wives were in advanced pregnancy upon departure from Gibraltar. So many births occurred at sea that amid the confusion a priest unaccountably recorded one birth as "parents unknown." But despite the many births, only 1,255 colonists arrived at New Smyrna, named by Turnbull in honor of his wife's birthplace.

In the meantime, however, the slave ship had gone down at sea with both living cargo and crew. And so the colonists, who had signed a contract obligating them to work for Turnbull for ten years on a share basis, were put to work clearing the forest as soon as they could build palmetto shacks for shelter. The climate was humid and hot, but the nights did not cool off as in the Mediterranean. Sickness, particularly malaria, took a toll; but many may have died from plain misery. For the colonists found themselves under overseers who had been accustomed to working slaves, or who had been noncommissioned officers in the British army. Floggings were common, as testimony later revealed, even when the colonists were ill.

A more motley group, with such a diverse background, was never brought to America, according to Leonard Usina, president of the People's First National Bank of Miami Shores, who proudly traces his ancestors to the Minorcans.

"Their blood was a cross-section of the centuries of hardy traders, plunderers and political firebrands of the Mediterranean," said Usina, "beginning with the Phoenicians and including the Greeks, Romans, Carthaginians, Vandals, Visigoths, and the Moors.

"Minorca long had been a convenient place for the exile of Castilian and Catalan trouble-makers, and the blood of these hot-headed revolutionists flowed through the veins of many Minorcans. Moreover, the group that came to America spoke three languages—a dialect of Catalan, Greek, and Italian. Even under ideal conditions, Turnbull and his backers might have had a difficult time establishing a successful colony."

The colony lasted nine years. The fewer than 500 who survived—they were described as demoralized, ill, hungry, and rebellious—abandoned their palmetto shacks and trekked to Saint Augustine. Turnbull's venture had cost 964 lives and 40,000 pounds sterling, equivalent to several million dollars in today's values. Disillusioned, Turnbull departed for Charleston, South Carolina, where he gained prominence as a physician.

The colony apparently thrived during its early years, despite the mood of the settlers and the brutality of the overseers. Returns from the shipments of the blue dye, indigo, in 1771 amounted to 13,500 pounds sterling, according to records of the British Board of Trade. Turnbull himself may have been a poor administrator. He appears to have shown little concern for the plight of his colonists and refused to hear their complaints. His temperament is reflected in his involvement in intrigue with other planters to have the governor of Florida, Patrick Tonyn, recalled. But trouble-makers there were from the beginning, and they persisted until the colony broke up.

In 1777, while Turnbull was in London seeking to have Governor Tonyn recalled, three colonists got permission to row across the Mosquito Lagoon and hunt for turtles on the ocean beach. Out of sight of the settlement, the three turned their boat north and rowed to Saint Augustine. There they went to Governor Tonyn, who, knowing Turnbull was in London trying to have him recalled, listened sympathetically to accounts of brutality and how colonists had been forced to eat snakes and "other vermin" to keep from starving. When Turnbull returned, unsuccessful in his quest to undermine Tonyn, he discovered New Smyrna deserted. The colonists had fled to Saint Augustine.

For a time the colonists lived in palmetto shacks on the northern outskirts of Saint Augustine, where conditions were about as miserable as what they had experienced in New Smyrna. Earning a living by farming and fishing, however, most of the colony managed to survive until the British ceded Florida back to Spain in 1783. This was a break for the Minorcans, who quickly moved into the houses abandoned by the British. And, being Catholic, the Minorcans fared well under the Spanish. A Minorcan priest, Father Campos, was given a chapel on St. George Street, not far from the city gate. Minorcans quickly became leading merchants and shippers. They dominated the fishing industry and became the leading farmers, providing most of the food for the Spanish garrison. And after the United States purchased Florida from Spain in 1821 the Minorcans became even stronger. They claimed nearly 50,000 acres of Florida lands. Many Minorcans became wealthy.

Minorcans have scattered throughout Florida. In addition to banker Usina, one of Miami's top businessmen, Edward N. Claughton, Jr., is a descendant of the Minorcans. His Minorcan blood comes from his mother, the former Lillian Corbett of Saint Augustine. In the Saint Augustine telephone directory are a dozen familiar Minorcan names—Pellicer, Manucy, Usina, Hernandez, Baya, Masters (for Maestre), Ponce (for Pons), Andrews (for Andreu), Leonardi, Pacetti, Capo, Pappy. Some are of Spanish, some of Italian, some of Greek, some of French descent. X. L. Pellicer, Sr., a banker, has been among the old city's important civic leaders for nearly half a century. Albert Manucy, a historian with the National Park Service, is an authority on Saint Augustine's Spanish architecture. W. I. Drysdale owns the Saint Augustine Alligator Farm. Emory J. Pacetti owns Marty's Restaurant. Dan Mickler has served as chairman of the county commission, while J. Earl Mickler has served as mayor of Saint Augustine.

And, in the meantime, what happened to New Smyrna? It remained abandoned until 1803 when Spanish land grants attracted new settlers, among them Minorcans from Saint

Augustine. After Florida became a United States possession, a group of New Yorkers operated a large sugar plantation west of town and built a sugar mill whose ruins, now owned and protected by the Florida Park Service, still stand. These ruins, as well as the ruins of a Spanish mission, have been wrongly accredited to the Minorcan colony. But the Minorcans remain, although they are becoming widely scattered, and that's more than can be said for those who left other relics—the original Florida Indians, the Spanish, or the British. They departed long ago, the Indians to oblivion, the Spanish back to Spain, the British to the Bahamas or to other British colonies. The Minorcans stayed to become more picturesque assets than any ruins.

SIX

How Vero Grew

Vero Gifford almost got cheated out of having her name immortalized as part of Vero Beach because of a rift between her husband and Florida East Coast Railway officials. John T. Gifford, former sheriff of Royalton, Vermont, moved his family to Florida in 1888 and settled on the west side of Indian River. Here a half-mile sand ridge separated the river from the endless marsh in the west. Gifford built a house. He cleared a hammock and planted citrus in the rich soil, as other Indian River settlers were doing. In 1891 Gifford asked the Post Office Department for permission to establish a post office. When the request was granted Gifford needed a name. He selected his wife's, Vero.

A year later, after Flagler had decided to extend his railroad from Daytona Beach to Palm Beach, his buyers called on Gifford. Most landowners were pleased enough with the idea of having a railroad that they gave right-of-way or sold it at a reasonable price. But Gifford, a hard bargainer, demanded and got a top price for his land. The stern, humorless New Englander then had words with the surveyors and the right-of-way clearing party.

The track reached Fort Pierce, twenty miles south of Vero, in January, 1894. But the trains didn't stop at Vero; they stopped at a labor camp two miles north. The mail was caught "on the fly," at Vero, and even freight, unless too large and fragile, was thrown from moving trains. Mockingly, the surveyors named the labor camp "Gifford," and the FEC built a depot here. Vero was designated as "Tie-pile near Milepost 228." Anyone from Vero wanting to catch a train had to hoof it two miles to Gifford, or get someone to haul him on a wagon; and passengers bound for Vero found themselves let off at Gifford, baggage and all.

To attract settlers to Vero, Gifford offered an acre of land to anyone who would agree to build a ten-by-ten shack. In time Vero had enough settlers that the Flagler people called a halt to the circus. Carpenters were sent to build a depot and paint it FEC yellow. Still, Vero lacked tourist appeal. Flagler's trainloads of cold Yankees headed on south, giving Vero on the picturesque Indian River only a bored glance.

Then one day in 1910 a millionaire from Davenport, Iowa, did stop at Vero. He was Herman J. Zeuch (pronounced Zie), founder of the Morris Plan banks. He also was a big-time food broker and an owner of many valuable properties. He didn't have to earn another penny the rest of his life; he already was living on Easy Street. But Zeuch, only forty-two, was a restless man who delighted in making money. He had developed communities in the West and in Canada. Now he was looking for another place to develop—maybe he could find it in Florida. An acquaintance, E. Nelson Fells, had just purchased more than 100,000 acres of marsh twenty-five miles northwest of Vero, which he was draining and subdividing into farms and groves. Meanwhile, in south Florida, the state was about to complete the drainage of the Everglades, which had been started in 1905. The Florida land fever had spread through the Midwest. Zeuch wanted to get in while the fever was high and there was still land to develop and sell.

Stepping off the train, Zeuch looked across the wet flat-woods and swamp west of Vero with a speculator's appraisal. All this country needed, Zeuch thought, was drainage. If a man could buy this swamp cheap and get the water off the land he could sell it off in small farm tracts and make millions. He knew this was what Fells was planning to do with the wet marshes he had bought. Zeuch had not seen Fellsmere Farms, but Fells was a famous engineer, having once worked for the Czar of Russia. If Fells could drain Fellsmere Farms, and if the state could drain the Everglades, then, Zeuch reasoned, he could drain and develop a Florida swamp too.

Hiring a horse and a guide, Zeuch took leave of Vero and splashed westward through the wet marsh. Three miles from the railroad track his guide led him into a hammock where Eli Walker had an orange and grapefruit grove. Here the land was only two or three feet higher than the surrounding marsh but the citrus was thriving. Sampling an orange, Zeuch swore he had never tasted one so delicious.

"What kind of orange is this?" he asked Walker.

"Indian River orange," replied Walker.

"What if you drained all this country; could you grow oranges on it?" asked Zeuch.

"Sure could," replied Walker. "Land's perfect for citrus—sandy, with a lot of humus."

Getting back on his horse, Zeuch returned to Vero. He wasted no time in slapping down an option to buy 50,000 acres at one dollar an acre, provided engineers found drainage feasible. Then he got a Daytona engineering firm to send an engineer to make a study. The engineer, R. D. Carter, was

almost as new in Florida as Zeuch, having only recently arrived from Hendersonville, North Carolina, where his last big
job was laying out Laurel Park, a mountain summer resort
community. Like many another engineer of that period,
Carter had a lot to learn about the flat terrain of Florida and
the tendency of dry years and wet years to come in cycles.
He reported to Zeuch that drainage was feasible and estimated the cost at $100,000. Zeuch hired Carter to take
charge, and in 1911 work was begun on the development of
Indian River Farms.

Carter cut a main canal, which is still called Main Canal. It
goes right through the middle of present day Vero Beach. To
Main Canal lateral canals were connected at every mile, and
these canals in turn were crossed by other canals at every
mile. By the time Carter had checkerboarded 42,000 acres
with canals the cost had reached $300,000.

"Why didn't you tell me it was going to cost $300,000?"
asked the irritated Zeuch.

"Because," replied Carter, "if I had given you the larger
figure to begin with you would have backed out of the deal."

Fortunate for Zeuch's real estate promotion and sales, the
years between 1911 and 1915 were dry years, or "normal"
years. Zeuch began advertising grove sites in the Midwest—
from ten to as many acres as you wanted. By the time prospects began arriving the water had drained from the marsh
between the mainland and Walker's Hammock. Walker's
orange crop Zeuch bought and prospects were taken out to
the grove where they were given fruit to sample. And Zeuch
had no trouble selling land for thirty to three hundred and
fifty dollars an acre, depending on the location.

Meanwhile, Fells was selling off his nearby Fellsmere Farms
in ten to forty acre tracts. He had cut a broad canal twelve
miles from the Saint Johns River marshes to the Sebastian
River to drain the land, and during the early years of development drainage was no problem. Thousands came and bought

property, and by 1915 close to 1,500 families had arrived to take possession of their "farms," build homes and plant citrus and vegetable crops. Then, in July, 1915, it began to rain. Nothing very serious at first. The canals engineers Fells and Carter had designed were taking the water away. But on August 3 a wet tropical storm passed offshore and sixteen inches fell on the land. Both Fellsmere Farms and Indian River Farms were flooded.

A young surveyor who helped lay out Fellsmere Farms, Herbert C. Watts, would remember half a century later that there was "some consternation."

"But we hadn't seen anything yet," he said. "While we were assessing the problem of how to hasten the drainage, a sheet of water was moving into the marshes from the central Florida highlands, and as it settled down upon us we were overwhelmed."

You could fish in the streets of Fellsmere, designed as the metropolis of Fells' development. The drainage canals meant nothing. You couldn't even see them. The countryside was a lake as far as you could see. Many farms were under five feet of water. Hundreds of cattle drowned as water reached windowsill level. Young citrus trees were covered completely with the black water. As soon as the settlers could dry out their clothes most of them boarded the train and departed from Fellsmere forever. It was a familiar Florida story. Many had sold their farms and their homes in other states to move to the new-found paradise. Fells went broke, but Fellsmere miraculously has survived. The drainage has been improved many times during the past half century, with the widening and deepening of canals and the building of a levee to keep flood waters from the west from rolling over the town.

Although Zeuch's Indian River Farms were flooded, and many of the planters departed from Florida, the enterprise survived. Carter raised a levee along the western border of the wet farms and installed more powerful pumping facilities.

Those who stuck it out developed one of the richest grove areas in Florida, and many of them became well off. And, as it happened, the project was a life-saver for Zeuch. His Morris Plan banks and food brokerage business folded during the depression of the thirties, and Zeuch would have wound up a pauper had it not been for his Florida properties.

It is doubtful that you would find many residents of Vero Beach today ("Beach" was added in 1925) who know a thing about Herman J. Zeuch, and only a small percentage of the sprawling city's 35,000 residents would have heard of John T. Gifford. But everybody knows of the legendary character, Waldo Sexton, who came to Vero in 1914 from Tailholt, Indiana, to help Zeuch sell farm sites. He also "sold" himself on the area, for he bought land, built a house, planted a grove, and started a ranch. But while waiting on the trees to fruit and the cows to calve, the restless Sexton needed something to do, so he began collecting "junk." At least it was junk to others. To Sexton the things he collected were "works of art"—unusual pieces of flotsam he found along the beach, as well as "antiques" he found in those places that called themselves antique shops. He liked to tell about the pair of lamps he bought from an antique dealer who claimed they came from a famous bordello in Saint Louis. He filled his house with the stuff he bought, much to the displeasure of his wife, who did not share his delight for collecting. What he couldn't get in the house he stored in a barn, while the statuary, carvings, old anchors, bells, wagon wheels, and countless other things that could take the weather were piled in the yard. Had Sexton been just a collector he would be remembered only as the eccentric junk man, if he were remembered at all. Imaginative, humorous, and having a bizarre artistic talent, Sexton turned his junk into fantastic monuments—the Driftwood Inn and Ocean Grille on the beach, the Patio Restaurant in downtown Vero, and "Sexton's Mountain," a forty-five foot high Azteclike pile Sexton left standing a couple of blocks from the beach. The McKee Jungle Garden, south of town on U.S. Highway 1, also was built by Sexton, but that had nothing to do with junk collecting.

I used to lunch with Sexton at the Ocean Grille when I would be visiting or passing through Vero Beach on a trip for *The Miami Herald.* In his seventies, he liked to reminisce and tell tall tales. The Ocean Grille, which could be called Driftwood Grille just as well, is a unique and interesting place, but it is the Driftwood Inn that's bizarre. Upon walking through this structure you are certain that whoever built it was out of his mind. You either like the Driftwood or you hate it. There's no in-between. But no matter how you view the Driftwood, you are impressed by the diverse collection of junk and you wonder where anyone could have found such a variety of everything from Baroque to "Early Pullman."

Sexton liked to tell you that the Driftwood Inn originally was a weatherbeaten mule barn, which he had moved, board by board and pole by pole, from his ranch.

"It was put up as a shelter for my family, whenever we went to the beach," said Sexton. "But people complained. 'Waldo,' they said, 'you can't leave an ugly thing like that on the beach.' Well, I didn't think the old barn was ugly; I thought it was beautiful. With its weatherbeaten and sun-bleached boards, I thought it looked like something built of driftwood. 'Waldo,' I said to myself, 'you've got something great. You can't tear that down.' "

So, in "improving" the mule barn, Sexton built a cottage. But he never stopped expanding as he collected more junk. In time he had a hotel—the Driftwood Inn. Meanwhile the depression of the thirties arrived, and at Palm Beach they began dismantling those enormous Spanish-styled mansions designed by Addison Mizner, an architect who was within one step of being as bizarre as Sexton. These houses were fantastic, and so were their decorations and furnishings. Sexton bought old lumber, doors, windows, grillwork, bells—Mizner

was a nut for collecting bells—as well as wood carvings, statuary, and paintings, which he hauled up to Vero Beach by the
truckload. When he sought to buy all the "junk" that came
out of one mansion, the contractor asked Sexton to pay
$5,000 for it.

"This stuff is works of art," said the contractor. "Mizner
brought it all from Spain."

"Art, hell," retorted Sexton. "Mizner made all this stuff
himself—or had it made—right here in Palm Beach."

Sexton wound up getting everything for a hundred dollars.
provided he would "haul it all away."

One day while having lunch with Sexton at his Ocean Grille
Restaurant, my eyes fell upon an antique door framed by
boards painted in the most indescribable blue I had ever seen.
These boards obviously had been used before. You could see
the old nail holes, and there were unpainted patterns that
remained after the boards had been torn from their original
setting. The blue color was intriguing. I asked Sexton where
he got those boards. Never one to give you a direct answer,
Sexton preferred to let you find the answer in the story he
related.

"People," he said, "are always saying to me, 'Waldo, why
are you so stingy that you won't finish painting those
boards?' I have to explain that those boards came out of
Addison Mizner's study in Palm Beach, and that there's no
blue paint in the world that would match the paint that's on
them. That's real Mizner blue."

When a dredge operator needed a place to dump some fill,
Sexton said, "Just dump it here." The "here" was a lot Sexton owned a few blocks north of his Ocean Grille. An idea had
just popped into Sexton's head: Vero Beach needed a mountain, and he would build one. But now that he had his mountain, Sexton's mind kept operating. "Why not decorate it,"
he thought. And so he did, building steps to the top and

covering them with Spanish tiles. He then paved the top with slabs of concrete lifted from an old water tower. The tiles that covered the slab and stairs came from the Edward Stotesbury mansion in Palm Beach. The guard rail about the slab was built from sections of the balcony of the old Windsor Hotel in Jacksonville. From the middle of the slab Sexton mounted an Indian totem pole, made of a fifteen-foot timber from an old railroad bridge. In front of Waldo's Needle, as the spire became known, Sexton placed two chairs, the "king's chair" on the right and the "queen's chair" on the left.

A team from the United States Geodetic Survey came through, measured Sexton's Mountain and pronounced it "the highest point between Kitty Hawk, North Carolina, and Key West." Before the beach area began booming in the 1960s, you had a regal view of the Atlantic from the king's and queen's chairs atop Sexton's Mountain. For a time the mountain, which looked like a cross between an Aztec temple and an orderly junk pile, was a tourist stopper. Sexton renamed it the Vero Beach Hanging Gardens. But after his death in 1968, at eighty-four, vandals began to lay waste to the Hanging Gardens, while collectors carried away bushels of the striking tiles. Weeds took over. Moreover, Sexton's family was having to pay taxes on what was becoming a civic eyesore. So Sexton's Mountain, or Vero Beach Hanging Gardens, was doomed. Sexton's Driftwood Inn and Ocean Grille also are doomed by time, or a hurricane. Vero Beach has had no hurricane since Sexton built these structures.

"Why should a hurricane bother us?" said Sexton, "It wouldn't have any challenge."

But his McKee Jungle Garden, a privately owned garden for which an admission charge is made, probably will survive. Only it doesn't have his name, but the name of the person who owned the site before Sexton took over.

Some years before his death, Vero Beach held a Waldo Sexton Day, or Screwball Day, to honor the city's most delightful personality.

"I'll admit I'm a screwball," said Sexton. "But I'm glad. I've had a lot of fun."

A good businessman, too, Sexton died a millionaire.

SEVEN

Ride on the Celestial Railroad

The fare for the seven and one-half mile trip from Jupiter to Juno was seventy-five cents, or ten cents a mile, but who could have complained about the price when the celestial journey took you by way of Venus and Mars?

Although nothing remains today of the Celestial Railroad except a few rusty spikes, like those collected from the abandoned roadbed by Mrs. John DuBois of Jupiter, its history is too fascinating to leave out of any collection of stories about the Florida east coast. The line, which connected Jupiter, southernmost port of the Indian River, with Juno, northernmost port on Lake Worth, was short-lived—from 1889 to 1895. But it left an imprint on the romantic lore associated with that period.

Built as the Jupiter & Lake Worth Railway, the line's sole reason for existence was the absence of a waterway across the

Bob Lamme

"peninsula" between Jupiter and Lake Worth. The Intra-coastal Waterway was not to be cut for another quarter-century, while in 1889 Flagler had not turned his eyes south of Daytona. River boats brought passengers and freight down the Indian River, which ended at its confluence with the Loxahatchee River at Jupiter. Here, almost under the shadow of the striking Jupiter Lighthouse, which is still in operation today, the passengers and freight were transferred to the J. & L. W. Line. The single engine, headed southward, made the journey to Juno in thirty minutes—when the engineer, Blus Rice, didn't stop to let passengers shoot at a deer or wild turkey. According to an advertisement in *The Tropical Sun* of Juno, southeast Florida's first newspaper, the train, with one passenger car and three freight cars, left Jupiter at 7:30 A.M. on the first of two daily round trips. It arrived at Venus at 7:45 A.M., Mars at 7:52 A.M., and Juno at 8 A.M. Since there was no way to turn around for the return trip, the little wood-burning, cabbage-headed engine backed its cars from Juno to Jupiter.

Miami played a role in the building of the Celestial Rail-road. In the 1880s Dade County extended north of the Loxa-hatchee River and included what is now Broward and Palm Beach counties as well as a part of Martin. Miami was the county seat, although only three houses stood about the mouth of the limpid Miami River. J. W. Ewan, known as the Duke of Dade, lived in a two-story house which had been built as an officers' quarters during the Third Seminole War of the 1850s. Nearby was a long, single-story building constructed of native limestone which had served as an enlisted men's barracks during the same period. Dade County paid the Duke—he was a native of Charleston, South Carolina—five dollars a month for the use of a room in the old barracks, where the county's business was conducted and court was held.

Ewan, a bachelor and one of the more colorful characters

among Dade County's early pioneers, arrived in Miami in
1874. He soon became the county's most influential person.
He served in the Florida Legislature, and was, at one time or
another, postmaster, county surveyor, deputy clerk of the
Circuit Court, notary public, inspector of customs, and
United States Commissioner. He also was a farmer and a real
estate developer. For a time he ran a store and for a brief
period operated the mail boat between Miami and Key West.
Courteous and scholarly, Ewan liked to quote from the clas-
sics, particularly the Latin and Greek scholars. But he also
was armed with a quick and cutting wit that often wounded
friends as well as enemies. The Cracker legislators dubbed
him the Duke of Dade, and the nickname stuck.

In 1888, Ewan raised the county's rent from five dollars to
fifteen dollars a month. A howl went up. Residents of the
Lake Worth region circulated a petition demanding a special
election, and got it. North Dade outvoted south Dade 107 to
eighty, and the county seat was moved from Miami to the
north end of Lake Worth. A two-story courthouse was built
and the name Juno—"bride of Jupiter"—was selected for the
new community.

At this time freight from Jupiter to Lake Worth was hauled
overland by oxteams, called bull trains. Persons traveling between Jupiter and the lake had a choice of riding the slow
bull trains or walking, which was faster. Plans to build a
railroad were discussed in 1887, but nothing happened until
Miami lost the county seat. Then promoters raised $70,000
and by July 4, 1889, the Celestial Railroad was in operation.
The bull trains went out of business. Charging 20 cents a
hundredweight for freight and a seventy-five-cent fare for
passengers, the line began to make money immediately. But
the railroad's biggest boom was yet to come.

In the meantime, Henry M. Flagler had extended his railway to Titusville, and in 1893 decided to extend it to Palm
Beach and build a huge hotel. But he wanted the hotel, the

Royal Poinciana, to be ready for opening upon arrival of the railroad. The only practical way to get supplies to Palm Beach was to boat them down Indian River to Jupiter and overland by way of the Celestial Railroad. The railroad collected $96,000 from Flagler during a few months' period, more than the cost of building the line.

Flagler got his revenge the next year when he bypassed the Jupiter-Juno peninsula with his line, dealing fatal blows not only to the Celestial Railroad but also to Dade's new county seat. The railroad ceased operating in 1895, at the same time that steamers suspended operations on Indian River and Lake Worth. Now Flagler had all the business.

Juno, left stranded without rail or steamer transportation, immediately went into decline. Most of the residents, now without jobs, moved away. Meanwhile, Mrs. Julia Tuttle, a widow from Cleveland, Ohio, purchased the property which the Duke of Dade had occupied, together with a square mile of what later would be downtown Miami. After the disastrous freezes during the winter of 1894-95 Mrs. Tuttle induced Flagler to extend his railroad to Miami. Miami was incorporated in 1896, and by 1899 south Dade voters were numerous enough to reclaim the county seat from Juno.

Weeds and grass grew up about Juno's abandoned wooden buildings, and woods fires burned them to the ground. The name survives in Juno Beach, a community some two miles north of the old site of the county seat. And what happened to Venus and Mars? Nothing. They never existed except in the imagination—being only names on sign posts along the line which Engineer Rice tooted his whistles at as he passed.

BOB LAMME

EIGHT

Playhouse for Millionaires

Those who know Worth Avenue, that street of haughty shops and restaurants in Palm Beach, associate its architectural spirit with Addison Mizner, eccentric genius of Florida's golden twenties. For it was Mizner who set the pace with the Everglades Club, together with several buildings he designed for shops and second-story apartments. On Via Mizner, an alley adjoining Worth Avenue, the architect raised his own apartment above an Old-World style patio. Standing in the patio and looking up, you can't help being impressed. The design—the lines and the way the structure towers above you—gives you something of an architectural thrill. And if you look near the foundation, among the shrubbery on the edge of the patio beneath the apartment, you will find a grave marker where Mizner buried his deceased pet monkey.

Mizner designed many of the mansions built by the rich at Palm Beach during the booming twenties—for the Phippses, Stotesburys, Dodges, Huttons, Posts. He charged enormous fees, and he was in so much demand that when Mr. and Mrs. Alfred G. Kay sought his services, he sketched a floor plan and elevation on a sheet of paper, handed it to them, and sent a bill for a full architect's fee.

Many of the opulent Mizner mansions, too big for human dimensions, were dismantled by the heirs and the valuable land divided into smaller parcels. But Mrs. Marjorie Merriweather Post has kept the 118-room Mar-A-Lago, with its seventy-foot tower, thirty-foot ceilings, and columned cloisters, together with the seventeen-acre tropical setting.

Mizner's greatest work, in his opinion, was the Cloister Inn, now the Boca Raton Club and Hotel, within view of Route A1A twenty-five miles south of Palm Beach. The Inn, where at one time only rich millionaires could stay, has undergone immense physical change since Addison Mizner and his brother, Wilson, opened it on February 6, 1926. Its successive owners have undergone even greater social change. Today a relatively poor man with only one yacht and one Cadillac can afford to vacation here. And all the reference he needs is a credit card.

Twice the hotel has undergone major expansions, and every successive addition has strayed further from Mizner's design. The last addition, done by Arvida Corporation, includes a modern high-rise. For a time it appeared that the tower would be the aesthetic death knell to Mizner's masterpiece, but now that a forest of other towers has risen about Lake Boca Raton, the original structure has returned to its own isolated independence, like Trinity Church among the highrises of Manhattan. Still, one is compelled to wonder how Mizner would react to the changes if he could see the "desecration" of his work. He probably would blow his three-hundred-pound stack. But Mizner has been dead since 1933, and Pennsylvania Railroad, which bought Arvida in the lush 1960s while it still had billions to spend, has not tooted a whistle of concern about what the controversial architect might think.

The original Cloister Inn was built at the height of the Florida land boom, when imaginative men walked among the clouds, and, like Greek and Latin poets, felt the warm breath of muses whispering in their ears. Some reached such heights of fantasy that they did the world a favor to come down to earth and walk with common men. Among the greatest of all out-of-this-world characters of that age was Addison Mizner. He was a tub of a man whose genius sparkled not just about his head but wreathed his enormous bulk in a kind of phosphorescent glow. At least that is the way Mizner thought of himself.

Mizner had arrived in Palm Beach a sick man during the winter of 1918. Recovering quickly in the tropical sunshine, Mizner reasoned that Palm Beach would be an ideal site to build a hospital for convalescing World War I veterans. He took the idea to Paris Singer, heir to a sewing machine fortune, who listened with expanding enthusiasm.

"Go ahead and draw the plans," said Singer. "We'll build it."

The walls for the monasterylike structure were going up when the war ended. Work stopped. No longer was there need for a hospital. Mizner and Singer got their heads together. Palm Beach needed an exclusive club. Could the structure be modified? It could. And, presto, the Everglades Club was born—one of the most exclusive clubs in the country, and still is.

Mizner's reputation was made. With Singer's backing, he began to transform Palm Beach with castlelike mansions. Every new one was more magnificent, more fantastic than the last. His confidence, a substance he possessed in abundance, grew into a comic opera kind of arrogance. Looking upon himself as architect, artist, decorator, carpenter, tile-maker, collector, critic, writer, raconteur, wit, Mizner knew there was nothing he couldn't do. It mattered none that he lacked an architect's degree. He made errors in drawings, and it was up to builders to catch and correct them. He would go through his scrapbooks, take details from photographs of Spanish, French, and Italian buildings until he came up with a complete house plan in a new and amazing design—an Addison Mizner creation. His services were in such demand during the mad days of the boom that he quit bothering to draw detailed plans. He merely sketched an idea and handed it to a builder. He might hand a mason the photograph of a Spanish fireplace with dimensions written on it and say: "Here, build this."

To furnish his buildings, he made raids on Spain with the help of no less a personage than the king. And Mizner was familiar enough with the king to call him "Alfonso." But when his demand for furniture, bric-a-brac, and art grew so great he could no longer supply it from Spain or Latin America, he made his own. He beat furniture with a chain to simulate age and fired a shotgun at wood to simulate worm holes.

Frank Lloyd Wright brushed Mizner off as a stage designer. Sculptor Jo Davison called him an architectural genius. Whatever the conflicting opinions, Mizner added his own dimension to the Mediterranean style of architecture which spread rampant through southeast Florida during the early twenties. But Mizner got bored with building for millionaires. He wanted to create his own world. And while he was in this mood his brother Wilson arrived in Palm Beach. Wilson Mizner, wit, opportunist, and rascal extraordinary, has been described by his contemporaries as a man nobody loved, not even his mother. He had a cruel sense of humor and the soft-minded cringed before his sharp barbs.

The Mizner brothers in 1925 acquired 17,500 acres at Boca

Raton, and Addison began to design the most fantastic community in America—described by a contemporary as a combi-
nation of Venice and Paradise—while Wilson dreamed only of
making millions. Lots went on sale May 1, 1925, and sales
reached $26 million within four months. The Mizners held
about $10 million in down payments. But the Mizner Devel-
opment Corporation planned to spend $200 million—mainly
other people's money. Among their backers was General T.
Coleman DuPont, among the nation's wealthiest men, and
Charles G. Dawes, vice president of the United States.

Addison turned the business end over to Wilson and turned
his attention to designing and building the Cloister Inn—the
most expensive 100-room hotel ever built. Wilson had charge
of promotion and sales, and he signed the checks. One day,
bored with writing small checks, he yelled at his secretary:

"I'm tired of putting my autograph on chicken feed; bring
me a million dollar check to sign."

To dignify his Cloister Inn, which was beginning to rise on
the west shore of Lake Boca Raton, Addison conceived the
fantastic Camino Real, wide enough for twenty lanes of traffic, with a Venice-like Grand Canal down the center. An
electric-operated Venetian gondola moved noiselessly up and
down the dark water. But by the time the Cloister Inn
opened in February, 1926, the boom was over, although
southeast Florida was to wait until a September hurricane
delivered the coup de grace.

Addison Mizner's fabulous inn was open but a few weeks.
When it closed its doors at the end of the 1926 winter season
the Mizner brothers were broke. After taking another look at
the fantastic razzle-dazzle the Mizners had dreamed up, their
creditors pulled the financial rug from under them. Addison
went back to Palm Beach, to his apartment on Via Mizner,
while Wilson departed for California, to join his friends in the
smoke-filled dives of San Francisco.

Now the truth was out. Irate buyers learned too late that

the Mizners had no money to live up to their promises of
making planned improvements. The brothers were sued. Wilson
son was brought back to Florida to testify. When a lawyer
asked him if he told a buyer he could grow nuts on the land,
Wilson replied from the witness stand:

"I did not tell this man he could grow nuts on that land; I
told him he could go nuts on the land."

The Mizners' skin was saved when the Central Equities
Company of Chicago, headed by Dawes and his brother,
Rufus, took over the Mizner Development Corporation. But
the practical Dawes brothers were hardly equal to the job of
running a Mizner fantasy. They sold in 1928 to Clarence H.
Geist, an uncouth millionaire from Philadelphia.

Contemporaries say that Geist, raised on an Indiana farm,
still had the smell of the cow barn about him when he built a
mansion in Palm Beach. He sat back and waited for an invitation
to become a member of the Everglades Club. When it
didn't come he was hurt. Then he got angry. He bought the
Cloister Inn. He would show Palm Beach a thing or two. He
would turn Mizner's creation into the most beautiful and
most luxurious private club in the world. Spending $3.5 million
on expansion, Geist added 300 rooms, several patios,
two swimming pools, dining rooms, including one for chauffeurs
and maids of guests. He built two golf courses and
employed Sam Snead, biggest name in golf of his day, as pro.
He built a cabana club on the beach and also quarters for 500
club employees. When the Boca Raton Club, as he called it,
was opened in 1930 it may well have been the world's most
luxurious, although not the most exclusive, since all you
needed to get in was a million dollars. A club membership
cost $5,000.

Club members enjoyed cloistered seclusion. No newspaper
reporter saw the interior so long as the club was under Geist's
control. For one reason, Geist had a chilling fear of being
kidnapped and held for ransom during that era when Dillin-

ger, Bonnie and Clyde, and the Barker family were on the rampage. Geist refused to have his picture made. None exists today. But he made sure that new guests knew him.

"I'm Mr. Geist, the owner of this club," he would say after tapping a guest with his walking stick. "Who are you?"

In the fall when Geist arrived at Boca Raton in his private railroad car he expected the townsfolk to be on hand to greet him—and they were because most of the townsfolk worked for him. Geist ran the town politically. He had the town charter rewritten to change the election date for town officials from November to February, when his full club staff was on hand to vote. It did not matter if they were not necessarily Boca Raton citizens—or even American citizens.

His affection for his club was so great that Geist left it $100,000 a year for five years after his death, which occurred in 1938. This was just long enough to keep the club going until World War II when the Army Air Corps took it over for a radar school. And so, until the war was over, the inside of the sprawling structure was off limits to the public just as it had been during the previous decade.

J. Myer Schine bought the club after the war, paying $3 million for the pile and its adjoining property. He added it to his hotel chain, and thereafter all you needed to get inside was a reservation and enough money to pay for your room and meals.

Among Schine's guests in the early fifties was millionaire Arthur Vining Davis, who had recently moved to Miami where he was living an exciting businessman's life by investing a million dollars a week in Florida real estate and in local corporations. Davis cast an envious eye on the Boca Raton Club and Hotel, as it had become known. In 1956 he asked the onetime Russian immigrant, Schine, if he wanted to sell. Schine did not—not for any price. But Schine ate his words when the 88-year-old Davis offered him $22.5 million for the property, which included 1,000 acres and several hundred feet of oceanfront. Now the owner of the hotel, Davis walked up to a bar and peered at bartender Jules Palabay, a native of the Philippines.

"Make me a martini—House of Lords—eight-to-one-and shake it," he ordered gruffly.

The personable Palabay mixed the martini, shook it, poured it in a polished martini glass—a large one—and set it before Davis, who sipped, raised his blue-gray eyes at the bartender.

"Now that's the way to make a martini," said the man who had just spent $22.5 million.

In 1958 Davis organized the Arvida Corporation ("Ar" for Arthur, "vi" for Vining, and "da" for Davis) and offered 49 percent of the stock to the public, which immediately bought it up like gold dollars selling for a dime. Davis died in 1962, and the administrators of his estate sold his 51 percent of Arvida stock to the Pennsylvania Railroad at a time when the company was on a buying jag. Pennsylvania poured new millions into a second major expansion of Mizner's creation.

The entrance to the Boca Raton Club and Hotel is perhaps more striking today than it was in the days of Mizner and Geist, because the palms lining Camino Real have matured. And also the muddy Grand Canal has been filled and now is a grassed parkway between traffic lanes. Entering Camino Real from U.S. Highway 1, you drive a mile along a superb winding boulevard of palms until you come to a circle. You go round the circle until you find yourself looking down a vista that carries your eyes to the massive entrance gate and to the hotel beyond. You take this avenue, lined by majestic royal palms, and drive to the gate, where your eyes are attacted to a bronze figure of cloven-footed Pan playing a pipe to welcome you. And now you see a guard standing in front of your car with the palm of his hand extended in your direction.

Are you a guest? Have you a reservation? Have you been invited? By whom?

You pass, if you convince the guard, and drive in between two balconied wings separated by a parklike setting of tropical foliage and colorful annual flowers.

You turn your car over to an attendant as the doorman looks you over, and you enter the main lobby. But if you are looking for Mizner's Cloister Inn you are in the wrong place. For this part of the hotel, with its red carpets and elaborately decorated architecture, was added by Geist, having been designed by Philadelphia architects who sought to outdo Addison Mizner. The entrance to Mizner's original Cloister Inn is in the east wing. As you approach the main entrance you will see it to your right.

Whether the Boca Raton Club and Hotel is good architecture is a question architects can settle. But there's something about Mizner's Cloister Inn that the architects who came later failed to catch—atmosphere. Mizner caught something of the Old World, but added his own originality in the decorated paneling and ceilings. A glance by the untrained eye is enough to separate Mizner's work from that of the architects who came later.

Among the fascinating details of Mizner's Cloister Inn were the "kidney-warmer" fireplaces. The beefy architect built several about the inn. On cool evenings he liked to stand with his back to the glowing coals. One of the kidney warmers has been preserved in a bar between the hotel's Patio Royale and the Cloister Loggia.

Arvida's addition rises from the southeast corner of the hotel, cutting off a wing of Mizner's inn; and guests have a choice of rooms from which they can look down on Lake Boca Raton or upon the red tiles of the not-so-modern Mizner-Geist creations. The new structure provides more comforts than Mizner or Geist ever dreamed of, but it lacks the Mizner air—an atmosphere that belongs to an era the like of which Florida is not likely to see again.

IN MEMORY OF
AMELIA,
WIFE OF
RALPH M. MUNROE
AND DAUGHTER OF
THOMAS HEWITT
OF NEW YORK CITY
BORN FEB. 7, 1856
DIED APRIL 2, 1882

BOB LAMME

NINE

Miami's Loneliest Grave

Near the entrance to the Coconut Grove Library, within sound of hundreds of footsteps daily, and near the almost constant roar of traffic on McFarlane Road, is the loneliest grave in the Miami area. Over it is a plain slab surrounded by a wrought-iron fence. The slab bears this inscription:

"In Memory of Eva Amelia, Wife of Ralph M. Munroe and daughter of Thomas Hewitt of New York City. Born Feb. 7, 1856. Died April 2, 1882."

One person in a thousand visiting the library knows the story behind this lone grave, although anyone who has lived in Coconut Grove any length of time knows the name of Munroe. Commodore Ralph Munroe, a former Staten Island manufacturer, boat designer, and boat builder, settled in Coconut Grove in 1885. He was a founder of the Biscayne Bay Yacht Club and was the club's first commodore.

Munroe built a house in Coconut Grove, facing Biscayne Bay, in 1891. The house still stands, and a son, Wirth, lived there until his death in 1968. Wirth's mother was Commodore Munroe's second wife, whom he married after settling in Coconut Grove..

The Commodore's first wife was the unfortunate Eva Amelia Hewitt. She and Munroe were married in Clifton, New Jersey, on July 16, 1879. Two years later, after she had given birth to a daughter, it was discovered that Eva Amelia had tuberculosis, which already affected her sister, Adeline.

It was at a time when a change in climate was thought to be the best treatment for tuberculosis. And Munroe, hoping to see his wife make a quick recovery, decided to take her and her sister to Florida.

Munroe had visited Biscayne Bay in 1877 at the invitation of William Brickell, who owned an Indian trading post at the mouth of the Miami River. He had met Brickell while in New York to buy supplies. Munroe was at this time unmarried and footloose, so he came down to Key West on a Mallory Line steamship and found a Conch, a native, to sail him through the Florida Keys to Biscayne Bay. He remained several weeks, becoming acquainted with such personalities of the frontier as Ned Pent, who made his living from the salvage of wrecked ships, and J. W. Ewan, better known as the Duke of Dade, who had arrived three years before to manage the properties of the Biscayne Bay Company, which then owned the land on the north side of the Miami River, now the central part of Miami.

Munroe's wife's illness brought back memories of the delightful climate of Florida and the beautiful, unspoiled Biscayne Bay. It should be an ideal place for her recovery. So, in the fall of 1881, Munroe hastily began making plans for the trip South, with the thought of spending the winter in Florida. He bought tents and supplies for five persons—for his wife and himself; her sister, Adeline; their brother, Thomas

Hewitt; and a nurse, Mrs. O'Dea. Leaving the Munroes' infant daughter with his mother, the party boarded a Mallory Line steamer for Key West. And on board Munroe arranged to have a thirty-foot shallow-draft sailboat, a Sharpie, transported.

At Key West the party transferred from the big ship to the sailboat and sailed through the Florida Keys to Biscayne Bay. They stopped at Cocoanut Grove (the correct spelling then) where Munroe already had made arrangements to rent a house from the Duke of Dade. But as Munroe reported in his book, *The Commodore's Story,* published many years later, the place was so lonely—being a mile from the nearest human habitation—that the party decided to move to the Miami River. And here, on the north bank of the Miami River, the party in early 1882 pitched their white tents among tall coconut palms, in the vicinity of where the entrance to the Dupont Plaza Hotel is now located.

A few hundred yards to the west stood a two-building complex known as Fort Dallas. One, a two-story structure, served as headquarters for the Biscayne Bay Company. The Duke of Dade lived and had his office here. The Miami post office had also been here for a time, but just before Munroe's party arrived the Duke had turned the job over to Miss Alice Brickell, and the post office was now in the Brickell Trading Post, across the river. The other building, a long, single-story structure, served as the county seat of Dade County. It held the county clerk's office, and the county commissioners had their infrequent meetings here.

We know pretty nearly exactly where Munroe's party pitched its tents. For early in February, 1882, Adeline Hewitt wrote to a friend, Miss Mary L. Cutler, of Merrillsville, P.O., Franklin County, New York, and included a sketch of the campsite's location. The letter and the sketch miraculously have survived the perils of time. Even the coconut palms, planted many years before by unknown hands, were located in the sketch. The site was not far from a Calusa Indian mound, leveled in 1896 for the building of Henry M. Flagler's sprawling Royal Palm Hotel. The party had planted a garden, and there was a dock on the river's edge where Munroe kept his boat tied up. Miss Brickell didn't get around to canceling the letter until February 9. Because she had no cancellation stamp bearing a postmark, Miss Alice wrote "Miami, Fla., Feb. 9, 1882" next to the stamp and canceled the stamp with strokes of her pen.

Miss Hewitt, who signed the letter as "Addie," hinted that her sister was doing poorly. But the letter cannot be considered a melancholy one. Perhaps Addie Hewitt was so influenced by the delightful setting—the blue bay, the crystal-clear river, and the coming and going of the colorful Seminole Indians who traded at Brickell's—to become a victim of melancholy. But the sisters were in much worse condition from the disease they shared than the letter to Miss Cutler indicated.

It was many years later that Commodore Munroe got around to relating his experiences of that spring of 1882. He was then married a second time and living in Coconut Grove. He could have written more than he did, but what he did write evoked painful memories.

"I built a skiff," he wrote in *The Commodore's Story*, "and made some fishing trips, and the time passed, but not with pleasure, for neither Eva nor her sister improved. . . . A few weeks later we laid her [Eva] to rest, close by, and striking our camp, set sail for Key West and home."

By "close by" Munroe meant that Eva Amelia was buried near the campsite, probably where one of the Dupont Plaza parking lots is now located. For there was no cemetery in the area at that time.

Sailing to Key West, Munroe and his party boarded a Mallory Liner for the return trip to New York. But Adeline Hewitt, whose condition had been worsened by the exertions of her Florida experiences, was near death as the steamer entered New York harbor.

"Just as the steamer made fast to the wharf in New York." wrote Munroe, "Eva's sister Addie also died, and the sadness of our return was complete."

Not quite. Munroe was yet to learn that his daughter, Edith, had died during his absence.

The restless Munroe, haunted by the memories of his experiences in Florida, returned in 1885. He bought property in Coconut Grove, where he remained for the rest of his life.

In 1895 Munroe learned that Flagler would extend the Florida East Coast Railway from West Palm Beach to Miami and build a resort hotel on the Miami River on or near the site where Eva Amelia had been buried in 1882. In the intervening years the area about the mouth of the Miami River had remained much the same as it was when Munroe's party had struck camp for the return to New York. Munroe had seen no reason to disturb the remains of his wife. But now something had to be done.

Munroe got busy. He gave land on McFarlane Road for a Community Church and for a cemetery. Then he had the remains of Eva Amelia removed from the site on Miami River and transferred to the cemetery in Coconut Grove. A church was built nearby, but a community grew rapidly about the area and no other burials were made.

Subsequently, Munroe gave adjoining land for a library, and on the corner of McFarlane and Bayshore Drive he gave land for the Housekeeper's Club, the first woman's club in Florida. The church was later acquired by the American Legion, which used the building as a meeting place until just before World War II when it caught fire and burned. A newer American Legion building now occupies the site.

Some years ago, when the Coconut Grove Library Association deeded the old library site to the city of Miami, which agreed to build the present library, it was discovered that the line separating the American Legion property from the library association property passed midway through the grave site. In order for the city to gain possession of the grave, so that it could be preserved and maintained, five additional feet were acquired.

And there it stands, the oldest marked grave in Dade County. The grave also is one of the Miami area's oldest surviving connections with the past. Two other memorials are older—Cape Florida Lighthouse and that long building at old Fort Dallas which once served as county seat of Dade County. But, like Eva Amelia's grave, the building no longer stands on its original site. Many years ago the building was dismantled stone by stone and rebuilt in Miami's Lummus Park.

TEN

Captain, Shove Off

It was no mere coincidence that Miami suffered a recession in 1913, following the death of Henry Flagler from a fall on the marble floor of his Palm Beach mansion. For fifteen years the builder of the Florida East Coast Railway had spent millions in southeast Florida. His final big project, extending his railroad to Key West, had been completed in 1912. The passing of Miami's first big spender was sorely felt. Ten percent of the 12,000 population was without work. Even the county government was broke. County employees were paid by checks but they had to pay a discount of seven to ten percent to get them cashed. The county's account was overdrawn and bankers didn't know when they would get their money. But in 1914 Miami got itself another sugar daddy.

James E. Deering may not have been nearly so wealthy as the partner of John D. Rockefeller in the building of the

BOB LAMME

Standard Oil Company, but, like Flagler, he proved to be a big spender. And in 1914, when the vice president of International Harvester Company began building Villa Vizcaya, he was soon employing every able-bodied man in Miami who needed work.

The building of Deering's luxurious palace, the like of which most Americans had not seen this side of Europe, had an immense effect upon the growth and development of Miami. Stonecutters were imported from Italy, gardeners and technicians from Scotland, engineers, carpenters, and masons from the North. Deering gave work to more than one thousand Miamians. On mornings and evenings, six days a week for nearly three years, hundreds of bicycles were strung out along the Cocoanut Grove Road, as workmen rode to and from their jobs.

As early as 1911 James Deering had begun thinking about building a winter home in Miami. His father, William, the founder of William Deering & Company—merged with McCormick into International Harvester Company in 1902—had a winter home in Cocoanut Grove. (The Cocoanut Grove post office was established in 1873. The name was changed to Coconut Grove in 1922, and, in 1925, after the village became a part of expanding Miami, the post office became Coconut Grove Station, Miami.)

James' brother, Charles, already was developing an estate two miles north of Miami at Buena Vista, now the site of exclusive Bay Point estates. Charles cut waterways, built a horse barn and a cottage. A waterfowl fancier, he introduced exotic ducks, geese, and swans. He also sent naturalists about southern Florida and the West Indies in search of rare tropical trees and palms. But Charles abandoned Buena Vista and moved to Cutler, fifteen miles south of Miami. The noise of passing Florida East Coast trains had bothered him. He sought to get F.E.C. officials to order a stop to the blowing of whistles and the ringing of bells as passenger and freight

trains rattled through Buena Vista. Failing at this, he planted
a row of trees between his property and the railroad. When
this failed to stop the noise, he pulled up stakes and moved,
building a modest home—modest for a wealthy Deering—in
Cutler Hammock.

Brother James also intended to build a modest home. But
that was before he met a long-haired dandy with a French
goatee, Paul Chalfin, an interior decorator and art buff. Deering, a bachelor and not in the market for a wife, required a
place only large enough for his comforts and for the entertainment of his friends, which were few. His Chicago home
would continue to be his principal residence. He also had a
villa in Paris and maintained an apartment at the Carleton
House in New York. Because of the pressure of work, he had
little time to stay abroad, and he used his apartment only
when in New York on business. But he planned to retire in
1919 when he reached sixty.

Deering had in mind a Spanish type villa in a Florida setting. It would be two stories, with a garden and a view of the
bay. With his brother Charles, James went up and down Biscayne Bay looking over the available sites along the shore. He
liked best a densely wooded area in Brickell Hammock, a
mile south of downtown Miami. On the north the property
adjoined Villa Serena, winter estate of William Jennings
Bryan, Woodrow Wilson's secretary of state. But there was a
problem. The rock road linking Miami with Coconut Grove
cut through the forest where Deering wanted to build.

The property Deering wanted was owned by Maude Brickell, who, with her husband, William, had built Brickell's Trading Post at the mouth of the Miami River in the 1870s. The
Brickells had purchased 640 acres on the south side of the
river, including what was to become known as Brickell Hammock. In 1892, four years before the settlement of Miami,
Brickell hired a crew of Bahamans to chop and grub a tun-
nellike road through the tropical hardwood forest from

Miami River to Dinner Key. Brickell died in 1902 after being kicked in the head by a mule. In 1913 Deering bought sixty acres from Mrs. Brickell, after being given permission by the county commission to relocate the road, and subsequently acquired another 100 acres.

The James Deering story might be worth no more than a paragraph in the history of Miami had he never met Chalfin. Deering had a decorating problem in his Chicago house and called upon Elsie de Wolfe, known also as Lady Mendel, one of the famous interior decorators of her day. Unable to answer Deering's call herself, she sent Paul Chalfin, whom she recommended highly. Chalfin, a New Englander who had studied art in Europe and had taught art at Columbia, had superlative credentials. He was himself a fair painter. He knew the museums of Europe as well as a matron knows the bric-a-brac she dusts. Chalfin not only pleased the sensitive bachelor in solving his decorating problem, but Deering found him so informative—in painting, sculpture, architecture, landscape design, and interior decorating—that he invited him to dinner. Deering, too, was interested in the arts. His duties at International Harvester, however, had prevented him from becoming the connoisseur that he would have liked to be. His daily life was dull and unrewarding, except that he was accumulating millions of dollars, so he found Chalfin stimulating. And, too, Deering wanted to discuss with Chalfin his plans to build a winter home in Florida. He could not have suspected that his involvement with the arrogant and snobbish Chalfin would cost him many millions of dollars he had not intended to spend. For Deering's tastes were simple, and it is not likely he would have gone in for anything nearly so extravagant as Vizcaya, had not the irrepressible Chalfin captured his mind.

Chalfin began immediately to discourage the building of a Spanish style house in Florida. The climate was much different from that of Spain, he pointed out. A Spanish house, with its small windows, would be dark and cold in winter; dark, hot, and humid in the summer. Had Deering thought of the possibility of an Italian villa? It would be more open, and with such design could be tied intimately with the garden and the vistas Deering had in mind.

Chalfin visited Miami at Deering's invitation and together they walked over the Brickell site. By this time Deering had been persuaded to consider an Italian villa. In the summer of 1913 they toured Italy together, visiting villas dating back to the Renaissance, as well as magnificent baroque gardens of the seventeenth and eighteenth centuries. In Florence they met Diego Suarez, widely known landscape architect, then went to France to talk with F. Burrall Hoffman, Jr., an architect with studios in New York and Paris. So completely now did Deering trust the persuasive Chalfin that the design and building of his Miami villa was turned over to him.

Later that year Hoffman visited Miami with Chalfin, where they studied the Brickell Hammock site. Then they journeyed to Italy to study the villas in which Deering had shown an interest. By the time the plans appeared on the architect's drawing board, Deering's ideas about a simple villa had vanished.

Construction of the palace was begun in 1914 following the arrival of a trainload of equipment—huge boilers and steam engines to operate quarries and rock crushers; an engine, cars, and rails for a tram train; a sawmill; concrete mixers; a carload of shovels, picks, grubbing hoes; carpentry and masonry tools; wagons, carts, wheelbarrows; tons of dynamite; flatcars of structural steel; carloads of lumber for the building of temporary structures such as toolhouses as well as for the building of forms for concrete. By water came a dredge to make a channel and to fill low land. But even before the arrival of the train came the engineers and foremen to survey and clear a site for the palace and gardens, as well as a new route for the Cocoanut Grove Road. Among the early arrivals was a photographer, employed by Chalfin. He was to make an almost day-by-day record of construction progress. This record has been preserved. A photograph of the architect's model of the Deering palace appeared in *The Miami Herald* on June 18, 1914. The caption said the walls were "to rise to the height of a five-story building, though the mansion will contain only two stories." But the photograph and legend could give only a hint of what the elaborate palace and grounds would be like when completed.

World War I began in Europe during August, 1914. But Chalfin already had purchased much of the art and furnishings in France and Italy earlier in the year, at a cost of more than a million dollars. Fortunately, Italy did not enter the war until mid-1915, giving Chalfin an opportunity to import stonecutters. Deering moved into his palace just before Christmas of 1916, almost on the eve of the United States' entry into the war.

The cost of building Vizcaya has been estimated variously between $7 million and $15 million. The lower figure would have been a fantastic amount of money before World War I. Flagler's overseas railway extension from Miami to Key West cost only $20 million. Chalfin had all the money he needed in the construction of the palace, gardens, elaborate outbuildings, and surrounding walls. Included were the gatehouse, boathouse, homes for the chauffeur, superintendent, and chef; stables for horses and mules; a cow barn, poultry house, and greenhouses. These outbuildings were like small mansions themselves, designed to be fit for a king's attendants, as well as for a king's cattle.

The villa was not quite ready for Deering's occupancy when he arrived in Miami on December 16, 1916, in his private railway car. He had to check in at the Halcyon Hotel, downtown, but, after frantic efforts by Chalfin, the contractors, and the decorators, Deering was able to move in a couple of days before Christmas, in time to invite the Deering family to Christmas dinner.

Deering spent nine winters at Vizcaya, before dying in

1925 at sixty-six. He would arrive about December 15 and depart about March 15. All together Deering spent twenty-seven months in his palace. After his death Miamians believed and passed along all kinds of stories about the bachelor occupant of Vizcaya. He had lived at a time when rich men enjoyed the privileges of princes. No stories about him as an individual, or anything about his private life, appeared in the Miami newspapers. No reporter would have thought of calling Deering for an interview. This resulted in a distorted view of the man. Fantastic stories about parties lasting for a week, with dancing girls brought from New York, persist. The truth is that Deering entertained very little. Those beautiful women are a myth. Deering seemed not to be interested in women except in a social way. Except for his mother, he seldom had house guests. Deering was a shy, introverted man who had become known as "the silent one" in the International Harvester Company. Although he had an engineering background, having attended Massachusetts Institute of Technology, Deering, as a vice president, concentrated on the improvement of his company's sales. But he worked through channels emanating from his high office, without participating in conferences with sales executives at a lower level, as is the general practice within industry today.

Deering apparently looked upon Vizcaya as more like a museum than a home. And while Deering liked privacy, in Vizcaya he got no more than the King of England got in Buckingham Palace. More than a hundred persons were required to keep the palace and the formal gardens. Everywhere he turned there was a servant, an artisan, repairman, or gardener. And, although Deering spent only three months at Vizcaya each year, he contrived ways to "get away."

Deering's most popular "get away" place was Cape Florida, at the south end of Key Biscayne where he owned 400 acres. There he built a lodge, an informal place among the hundreds of coconut palms, little more than a stone's throw from the historic Cape Florida Lighthouse, which was on his property. Once or twice a week he boarded his motor launch, the *Fish Hawk,* and crossed Biscayne Bay to Cape Florida. At Vizcaya the gardens were kept in near perfect condition by two dozen gardeners. At Cape Florida he had only a caretaker, whose sole duty was to keep the lodge in order and shoo away curious sightseers. Otherwise nothing could be touched. Deering wanted everything left as nature shaped it. Palm fronds and coconuts were left where they fell. Nor could the weeds be cut because one could not do so without destroying the wildflowers. Deering liked to stroll among the coconuts and along the beach, often contemplating the picturesque lighthouse, completed in 1825, four years after Florida was ceded to the United States by Spain.

Although the lighthouse had not been in use since 1878, when its function was taken over by Carysfort Light on the Florida Reef, the ninety-five-foot tower had survived hurricanes, wars, and vandals. In 1836, during the Second Seminole War, the lighthouse was attacked by a band of Indians. The keeper, John W. B. Thompson, and his black assistant named Henry, escaped by climbing to the top and pulling the ladder up behind them. But the Indians built a huge fire that roared up the interior of the structure as if it had been a chimney. The two men, to escape being roasted, climbed outside and sought to protect themselves from Indian bullets by lying on a metal catwalk near the top. A Navy vessel from Key West arrived the next day to find Thompson alive but his helper dead. (The lighthouse is today preserved as a museum in the Cape Florida State Park.)

Living with Deering part of each winter was his mother, widowed after William Deering died in 1913. Like her son, Mrs. Deering found Vizcaya lonely, and she enjoyed going to Cape Florida, too. Deering took her on occasions, but preferred going alone. Moreover, she was slow and he had to wait on her. One morning he left her standing on the dock.

When planning a trip to Cape Florida, Deering informed his captain the day before so he would have the *Fish Hawk* at dockside. On this day he wanted to go alone, but his mother saw the launch as she entered the breakfast room.

"Oh, James," she said, "I want to go with you."

"All right" he replied, "but we sail at exactly 8:30."

After finishing breakfast, Deering pushed his chair from the table and looked at his watch.

"Mother," he said, "we sail in twenty minutes."

"All right, son, I'll be there," replied Mrs. Deering. After hastening through breakfast, Mrs. Deering went to her bedroom "to get a few things," but stayed and stayed. She was on her way to the dock as her son studied his watch.

"Captain, it's 8:31," he said. "Shove off."

And off the launch chugged, leaving Mrs. Deering on the dock. Her son never looked back.

A visitor to Vizcaya in the early twenties counted five twelve-cylinder Packard automobiles in Deering's garage. He added a new Packard every year, but the vehicles were used little and all looked new. Deering liked to be driven over his estate by his chauffeur, visiting the vegetable farm, the cut flower garden, the dairy, and the stables. He seldom visited homes in the area. He had a few friends among the "natives," but preferred to invite them to Vizcaya, or to a cookout at Soldier Key, in Biscayne Bay, which he rented.

After his death nobody in the Deering family wanted to live in Vizcaya. The maintenance of the estate was reduced to caretaking level, which meant that most of the hundred employees were paid off. Gradually the gardens declined and the outbuildings suffered from neglect. Seeing the decline worried the Deering family, and in the thirties the daughters of Charles Deering, Mrs. Chauncey McCormick and Mrs. Richard Danielson, took turns living there each winter. But it was depression times. The expenses were great and, also, living in Vizcaya was a lonely ordeal. The palace and gardens were opened to the public for a time, for a small fee, but this didn't pay and the gates were closed. So for several years, until the early fifties, Vizcaya stood deserted. The only ghosts were vandals, who climbed the walls or entered through the waterways. Statuary, carved from the local limestone by Italian artisans, was overturned and broken, while the delicate artwork about gates and fountains was removed or defaced.

The Deerings, in the meantime, sold off parts of the estate —one area for a subdivision and another for Mercy Hospital and a Catholic high school. Then, in 1952, the remaining thirty acres, including the palace, formal gardens, gatehouse and several other elaborate attendant buildings, were sold to Dade County for $1,050,000 while $1.5 million worth of furnishings and art were donated.

Vizcaya is now operated as a museum under the Dade County Parks and Recreation Department, which maintains the palace and the gardens as closely to their original splendor as possible. A guidebook suggests the visitor plan to spend at least two hours to see everything.

But while a visitor may admire and wonder at this extravagant monument to a rich man's whim, there's nothing about to give a picture of what the builder—the silent one—was really like.

ELEVEN

By Train to Key West

The drive from Miami to Key West on the overseas highway is a spectacular experience even after you have been the route countless times. For those who have little hope of repeating the trip, the drive might well be their most unforgettable Florida experience. But the trip by car cannot be compared with the trip my wife and I made in 1935 on the train that "went to sea."

We moved to Miami from Jacksonville in January of 1935. A month later we went to the old Florida East Coast Railway depot, almost within the shadow of the courthouse, and boarded a southbound train. It was Sunday, at the break of dawn. As I remember, the excursion fare was $2.50 apiece.

It was a sleepy crowd that boarded with us, and it was a reluctant and sleepy steam engine that chugged across the Miami River as we started out on our 160-mile trip. We were quick to learn the reason for the early hour of departure. The train stopped at every raccoon trail. We were at least an hour reaching Homestead, thirty miles down the track. And by the time we pulled out of Florida City, the southernmost mainland town, the holiday-bound passengers had become wide awake and impatient. This time the engine chugged for a considerable distance, through mangrove swamps and over causeways built across quiet bays and lagoons. Then we began making frequent stops again at the little settlements in the Keys. Sometimes there would be only a depot and a water tank. But there was always a group of people standing about, to "see the train come in." Here we would wait until the engine quenched its constant thirst, and, once more, with the shrill sounds of a whistle and the clanging of a bell, we would be on our way. The bridges began to get longer. We crossed one bridge that seemed to be a mile long. On the west a quiet bay was so shallow that a fisherman was poling his skiff, while on the east side the blue, choppy water extended to the horizon.

"That's the ocean," said a young woman. "We're crossing the sea."

"If that was the bridge over the ocean," said a middle-aged woman sitting across the aisle from us, "I'd like to show these people the Mississippi. We've got longer bridges across bayous out in Texas where I live."

The bridges got longer and longer as we progressed south, or, more correctly, west. For to reach Key West you travel south to Key Largo, then turn westerly. Eventually we reached a bridge so long it almost faded out of sight over the horizon ahead of us. This was the Seven-Mile Bridge. From the windows of the train we could see only blue water on either side. Had it not been for the slow clickety-clack of steel wheels on steel rails, I could have imagined myself on board a ship. We could have rowed on to Key West, if each passenger had been given an oar.

"By hoisting a sail," I thought, "we could sail to Key West."

It was nearly noon when we arrived at Key West. We got off the train and followed the crowd, ending at Duval Street. Everything was closed except a drugstore and a couple of eating places. Few people were to be seen. We spoke to a man whom we hoped to ask about Key West, but he answered in Spanish. At that time the majority of the island city's 12,000 population was either Latin or Conch. The Latins were descendants of the exiles who fled from Cuba before the Spanish-American War. The Conchs were descendants of Bahamans who came to Key West early in the nineteenth century as "wreckers"—hardy seamen who made their living by salvaging the cargo of wrecks on the treacherous Florida Reef.

We found ourselves strolling down the middle of the street, for there were no cars—only bicycles, and few of them on Sunday. We walked a mile to the Atlantic at the east end of Duval Street, then walked a mile back by way of back streets where we admired the old houses behind the green foliage of Spanish lime trees, palms, and frangipanis. Near Mallory Square we stopped at a Cuban outdoor restaurant, where the tables were set up on a tile deck, under a canopy of thatch, and here we ate thick Cuban sandwiches, drank colas, and tasted our first coconut ice cream. We killed the afternoon, until train time, visiting the Aquarium where we ogled the colorful fish, visiting the turtle kraals where the big sea turtles are held while awaiting buyers, and loafing about the docks where fishing boats were tied up. It was late and we were tired when the train left Key West. The sun was setting as we reached the Seven-Mile Bridge. It was a spectacular sight, the huge red sphere sinking into the water, like a glowing ball being slowly submerged. The sky faded as our train ambled on at a slow clickety-clack into the growing darkness.

How could we know this would be our last train trip to

Key West? Six months later a small but fierce hurricane crossed the Florida Straits and bore down on the Upper Keys. The center passed over Islamorada early in the night of September 2, trapping a Florida East Coast Railway passenger train sent to evacuate the area in the path of the storm. The hurricane's force was incredible. The barometric pressure at its center dropped to 26.36, one of the lowest recorded in a hurricane. With ten percent of the normal atmospheric pressure lifted from the sea, the surface in the storm's center rose like a bubble in a weak spot on an inflated balloon. As the storm approached, the low islands began to feel the encroachment of this "bubble of water," which came like a great tide. Driven by a fierce wind, estimated at 200 miles an hour, the water smashed everything on Upper and Lower Matecumbe that man had built, while the trees that remained standing were only sticks or poles on the morning after. More than twenty miles of railway bridges and causeways were washed away. Reporters and photographers, who reached the scene as soon as they could get across the wild tidal channels, were appalled by the death and destruction. Even the steel cars of the refugee train had been carried from the track, and would have been washed off Upper Matecumbe Key had they not lodged against debris. Only the heavy engine and tender remained on the track. More than 500 lost their lives, mainly on Upper and Lower Matecumbe.

The hardy survivors rebuilt their homes and the devastated tropical trees eventually came back. But the railroad was never rebuilt. The overseas extension, which Henry M. Flagler had completed in 1912, had never paid anyway. So the railroad south of Florida City was abandoned. During the next three years a highway was built over the old roadbed, across the viaducts and causeways, and in 1938 the Overseas Highway was opened.

During the nearly forty years since we first visited Key West, we have seen the city grow from 12,000 to more than

60,000. For a time it appeared that the old part of Key West would disappear altogether, under the pressure of developers, to be replaced by modern filling station and hamburger house architecture, with gaudy neon signs in place of the wonderful old houses, the trees, and the palms. But, old Key West hasn't disappeared. A few of the old houses were lost, but the loss awakened Key West citizens to the realization that their heritage was being destroyed. Battle was made against the rank, unconscionable monster called Progress. Even the Chamber of Commerce was enlisted on the side of preservation.

One of the most handsome of the old houses preserved is the Geiger House, built in the 1820s by Captain John H. Geiger, one of the early wreckers. When the Mississippi Valley was opening up in the early nineteenth century virtually all of the commerce between New Orleans and the East Coast was through the Florida Straits. This was before the railroads reached the Mississippi Valley, and hundreds of sailing vessels were needed to carry the vast amount of cargo—cotton and lumber to the East and to Europe, returning with rich cargo of necessities and luxuries. The federal government began a string of lighthouses along the reef between Cape Florida and Key West after Florida became a United States possession in 1821, but many years were necessary to complete the vital markers. In the meantime, countless vessels piled up on the reef. Key West drew Bahamas and New England skippers, like Geiger, Captain George Carey, and Captain Bradish Johnson. Johnson, the most successful of the wreckers, earned the title of "King of the Wreckers," and the nickname of "Hog" Johnson. These and other wreckers were licensed by the federal government. The cargoes they salvaged were taken to Key West and stored under federal lock and key, under the jurisdiction of the admiralty court, until sold at auction. The cuts received by the wreckers, plus what they could steal, made them rich. Key West prospered and a few, like William Curry, became millionaires.

Curry came to Key West from Green Turtle Cay in the Bahamas during the 1820s at fourteen. He was not a wrecker but a merchant. He made his money as a supplier for the wreckers. Curry built the largest home in Key West, but he needed something more special than just a big house to show off his wealth. So while in New York on a buying trip, he went around to Tiffany's and ordered a gold service for his table. The cost was $100,000. Years ago when I heard this story I thought it was another Key West tall tale. But a portion of Bill Curry's table service is now on exhibit in the Florida First National Bank in Key West. An armed guard stands nearby. The rest of the service has been scattered among Curry's descendants. Curry's house has been dismantled, as has the home of Hog Johnson. Captain Carey's house, built in the 1830s, still stands but is a private residence, the home of Mr. and Mrs. E. L. Newton. Mrs. Newton —Jessie Porter Newton—is the great-granddaughter of William Curry.

The irrepressible Mrs. Newton was responsible for preserving the Geiger house. A distant relation of Geiger had lived in the house for several years as a recluse. The structure had fallen into disrepair and the garden about it had become a wilderness. Mrs. Newton got word that an oil company was about to buy the house, which was on a corner, tear it down, bulldoze out the old trees, and build a filling station. She refused to believe this could happen. Here John J. Audubon had stayed while visiting Key West in the 1830s. Here he had painted the white-crowned pigeon, native to the Keys and the Bahamas. Mrs. Newton called Mitchell Wolfson in Miami. After having grown up in Key West, Wolfson had moved to Miami, to become the wealthy principal stockholder in Wometco Theaters, owner of television station WTVJ, and operator of the Seaquarium.

"Mitch," she said, "they're about to tear down the old Geiger house. You've got to buy it."

Wolfson did buy the old house, and he had it restored. Now a museum owned and operated by a nonprofit foundation set up by Wolfson, the house is open to the public for a fee, under the name of Audubon House.

You can get a location map and brochure "The Pelican Path," showing the interesting old places in Key West, from the Chamber of Commerce office at Mallory Square. But the best way for the green visitor to make a quick acquaintance with Key West is to take a ride on the Conch Train. It takes you through the old city and part of the new, as well as through the Naval Station, a base for nuclear submarines. A guide gives you a running account of the history behind what you see. After the trip, you know something of the island's colorful background, and you're better prepared to enjoy a walking tour of the old town.

Over the years my wife and I must have tramped a hundred miles through Key West's old streets, up and down Duval, Whitehead, Simonton, Front, Greene, Caroline, Fleming, Southard, Anglea, Elizabeth, William, Margaret—even as far as Francis, and Passover, the appropriately named street beyond which the City Cemetery lies. Yes, we have gone through the cemetery, as countless others have done. Some years ago we went there looking for the grave of Abe Sawyer, a colorful midget who in the 1920s and 1930s was a frequent sight in the streets of Miami and Coconut Grove. Colonel Sawyer, as he was called, was always nattily dressed. He sported a cane, wore his hat at a jaunty tilt, and smoked a full-sized cigar. In his high pitched voice, Colonel Sawyer could preach a moving sermon, as well as deliver a rousing speech on such patriotic occasions as the Fourth of July. He was crazy about the women, and they pretended to be crazy about him. He liked to escort them in the manner of a dandy. But when the circus came to town, Colonel Sawyer was not to be seen. He was afraid of being kidnaped and hauled off with the Big Top.

Well, after considerable looking, we found the grave. We

had expected to see a child-size grave. But, no. It was adult-size, covered with a granite slab. Somehow, on the way to the cemetery, Colonel Abe had received a boost in rank. On the grave slab was the following inscription:

"GENERAL ABE L. SAWYER, 1862-1939."

As I said the City Cemetery has had countless visitors. Many have gone there looking for an elaborate but empty tomb which onetime held the remains of a beautiful Key West girl, Elena Hoyos Mesa, who died in 1931 at twenty-two.

The tomb is not to be found, and those who wander through the cemetery looking for it failed to read the story completely. That story began in 1930 when an eccentric German, Karl Tanzler von Cosel, sixty, appeared in Key West and got a job as X-ray technician at the Marine Hospital. With his Vandyke beard, haughty manner, and penetrating stare, he passed himself off as a scientist—a mad scientist, some thought. He claimed to have been born a count, and said he possessed nine college degrees.

One day a young woman entered Von Cosel's X-ray rooms with an order to have a chest picture made. Although she was under treatment for tuberculosis, Elena Hoyos possessed a frail beauty that captivated the lonely, elderly man. Finding an excuse, he called upon her in the impoverished cottage of her parents. He returned time after time, always with presents—a ring, a watch, even a bed to replace the poor thing she was sleeping on. Then Von Cosel began talking of marriage. Elena gave him a polite rebuff but that failed to stop him. The months passed. Elena grew weaker. One night she had a seizure and died. She was buried in the City Cemetery. Von Cosel visited the grave daily. Then he went to the girl's parents and got permission to build a vault.

Von Cosel built one of the most elaborate mausoleums in the cemetery. Elena's casket was transferred to it. Prying open the lid, Von Cosel discovered that the body was disintegrating. Shocked, he sought to stop the decay with the use of embalming fluids. Daily he visited the mausoleum, going inside to kneel beside the casket and study the remains of the girl he had grown to love even more in death than in life. But, despite his constant efforts, the body still deterioriated. He moved it to the dilapidated shack where he lived on the edge of town. By this time the body was little more than bones and decay. But, setting to work with wire, plaster, and wax, Von Cosel rebuilt the body to a semblance of life. The manikin completed, he dressed it in a wedding gown and placed it on a canopied bed. And here, for the next several years, lay the remains of Elena Hoyos while her lover, in his fantastic imagination, experimented with an ultraviolet ray with which he hoped would regenerate life. For he believed the spirit of Elena Hoyos inhabited the manikin, and that it was possible, through science or magic, to discover a way to make it active again in the girl's body. He also worked on the chassis of an old airplane, in which he planned to fly the remains of Elena into the stratosphere, if the ultraviolet ray machine failed to work, and here he hoped the powerful rays from outer space would restore her life. In the evenings he sought to pacify Elena's spirit by playing soft music on an old pipe organ, which he had obtained from a church and rebuilt. Although he must have known she could not see, because her eyes were of glass, he believed her spirit could hear. And when he was not playing music he often talked to her spirit about his plans to fly her across the Atlantic to his castle in Germany.

In the meantime, Elena's sister, Mrs. Mario Medina, became suspicious that the elaborate tomb Von Cosel had built was empty. One day she went out to Von Cosel's shack while he was in town, peeped through a window, and discovered the truth. Von Cosel was arrested. The bizarre story appeared in newspapers throughout the country. Elena's body—or the manikin Von Cosel had created—was put on public view at the Lopez Funeral Home. In three days nearly 7,000 passed through in a continuous line to gaze at the painted wax features which bore a striking resemblance to the girl now nine years dead.

Meanwhile, Von Cosel had become famous. Interviewed by reporters, he told of his love for Elena and of his efforts to revive her. He pleaded that she be returned to him so he could continue his experiments. The romantic account of the seventy-one-year-old madman's love for a corpse gained a great deal of sympathy for him, because the authorities did not reveal the more lurid side of the story. And, to avoid having to do so at a trial, to the embarrassment of Elena's family and friends, Von Cosel was freed. Once again he sought permission from a judge to regain possession of his "beloved Elena." The judge refused.

At the request of Elena's sister, a group of friends took possession of the manikin, and buried the remains in an unmarked grave in the City Cemetery.

The bizarre story drew thousands of curious to Key West. So many appeared at Von Cosel's shack that he began charging admission and gave conducted tours, showing the things that people had read about in newspaper stories—the bridal bed, Elena's death mask, the pipe organ, a ray machine, and the plane with the name "Cts. Elaine Von Cosel" painted on the side. Eventually the owners of the property on which Von Cosel had his shack booted him out. And in April of 1941 he left Key West and moved to Zephyrhills, in central Florida. On the same night that he left town an explosion blew the empty mausoleum Von Cosel had built for Elena into smithereens. And that's why the curious who go to the City Cemetery looking for Elena's tomb are unable to find it. Nor can they find the unmarked grave that holds Elena's remains. All members of the group that were present on the night of the secret burial have died except one, Bienvenido Perez. He was still living in 1972, but, with his tongue paralyzed by a stroke, he could not talk. At last Elena Hoyos Mesa could rest in peace. And what happened to Von Cosel? He lived until 1952, dying at eighty-three.

Key West has attracted many colorful personalities, some of them bizarre—but none so bizarre as Von Cosel. Not the least of the colorful figures was Ernest Hemingway, who lived on Whitehead Street during most of the thirties. He wrote the greater part of *For Whom the Bell Tolls* here. Many Hemingway admirers come to Key West in hope of catching a glimpse of the scene and experiencing a glow of the atmosphere of those years when "Papa" lived and wrote and drank here. Hemingway buffs usually drop into Sloppy Joe's at Duval and Greene Streets. But if you want to drink like Hemingway, you'll have to order Teacher's Scotch or a martini on the rocks. The Hemingway martini is made by filling a short glass with ice cubes, adding half a bottle cap of dry vermouth and a cocktail onion, then floating the ice with gin. (Some call it a gibson, but to Hemingway it was a martini.)

To follow the Hemingway circuit, you should first drop in at Tony's Saloon, half a block away on Greene Street. For this was the first location of Sloppy Joe's. But wherever you go, the atmosphere will be a lot different from the Hemingway days when the saloons were filled with commercial fishermen and fishing guides. Now Sloppy Joe's and Tony's Saloon are likely to be filled with hippie types who like loud juke-box music and songs by Tom Jones.

But if you leave Mallory Square behind and take Whitehead Street, past the quaint old Coast Guard Building and the Old Post Office, past the Audubon House, with the Naval Station fence on the right—beyond the fence is the Bahama-shuttered Little White House where Truman vacationed—you eventually arrive at the Hemingway House at 907 Whitehead. You have walked nine blocks through the area which has changed very little since the days Hemingway lived here. For a brief moment, as you study the house, almost in the shadow of the old Key West Lighthouse which stands among a grove of coconut palms across the street, you might feel that you have caught a bit of atmosphere Papa knew and which the citizens of Key West are trying to preserve.

TWELVE

By Oxcart Across the Everglades

During the dry spring of 1910 the Ox-Woman hitched her pair of scrawny oxen to a cart in which she had loaded her meager belongings and started out across the Everglades on the most remarkable trip we have any accounts of in southern Florida.

Sarah Smith McLain, six feet four and as strong as a field hand, had arrived in Dade County five years before, driving a pair of oxen from her home in Racepond, near Folkston, Georgia. She worked for a time on the farm of W. B. Focht near Goulds, grubbing palmettos, hauling limestone rock, and plowing. A sister of Mrs. Focht, Mrs. John L. Murray, recalled that the huge woman would sit on the porch of the Focht home in the evenings, singing "Barbara Allen" and other songs of that period.

"She told us that she had been married at sixteen," said

Mrs. Murray, "and that her husband had been hanged in Folkston after being convicted of killing a man. To earn a living, she ran a crosstie camp for awhile, then operated a barbershop in Waycross. I remember her saying she could 'shave a man three days under the skin.' She had only two dresses and a black sunbonnet. And she wore men's work shoes."

She carried a shotgun resting against the seat beside her as she drove her cart through the countryside. Her cart was always followed by two hounds as scrawny as her oxen.

"In Miami she was a great curiosity, and people came out of their homes and business places to see her," said Mrs. Murray. "She usually camped where night caught her, but she had a way of making friends, and people never seemed to mind putting her up. She refused to sleep in a bed, preferring a pallet on the floor. Everybody referred to her as the Ox-Woman."

Remarkably, Sarah McLain had three giant sisters like herself. Nancy Smith, called "Big Nancy," and Hannah, called "Big Six," never married. Both could cut crossties and chip "catfaces" on pine trees for turpentine gum as well as any man. Lydia, an illiterate who signed her name with an X, was the money-maker. She contracted the cutting of crossties for railroads and operated a turpentine still. She also owned cattle and traded land. Old-time residents at Racepond remember that Lydia married a normal-sized man. She would sit in a rocker on her front porch, holding her husband in her arms and singing love songs to him. The giants' father, Pappy Smith, was described as the "biggest man in south Georgia." He had three other daughters of normal size, who married and raised families. None of the four giants had children.

Mrs. McLain lived five years in Dade County. After working a season for the Fochts, she set up camp on a key in what is now part of the Everglades National Park and farmed a glade during the dry season when the water was off the land. She also hunted deer and peddled the venison among the farmers and grove owners of south Dade. At other times she would buy a steer, butcher it, and peddle the meat from house to house.

In 1909 the Ox-Woman received a letter from her family in Racepond advising her that her younger sister, Hannah, had left home and was living at the town of Everglades. Would Sadie, as her family called her, check on Hannah and see if everything was all right? Inquiring, she learned that the place where Hannah lived was "t'other side of Florida," seventy-five miles distant, beyond the sawgrass-covered Everglades and Big Cypress Swamp. No highway across southern Florida existed. To reach Hannah, the Ox-Woman would have to drive her oxen north to Melbourne, cross the state to Tampa, then travel south to Fort Myers. There she would have to take a boat. It was a distance of more than 300 slow miles and would take two or three months. Even with the prospects of hardships, the direct route seemed preferable. All the Ox-Woman needed was a dry spring, when the Everglades and swamps normally dried up to ponds and sloughs. Moreover, the Everglades was burned virtually every year, or, if necessary, she would set fire to the sawgrass ahead of her to clear a way.

The year Mrs. McLain planned her trip across the Everglades was just before the opening of a system of canals, started in 1905, which would drain this vast River of Grass, as the Indians called it, forty to sixty miles wide and extending from Lake Okeechobee to the mangrove swamps of Shark River and Florida Bay. For centuries before the arrival of the white man the Florida Indians had used the Everglades as a waterway for their dugout canoes. Summer and fall rains filled the glades with one to three feet of water, and in the late fall and early winter Indians poled canoes from as far as the Saint Johns River—through the Saint Johns marshes, across Hungryland Slough, and down the broad River of

Grass. They made their camps on the countless Everglades tree islands, from which they hunted for several weeks before returning home with skins of deer and otter and dried venison. South Florida was then as close to a paradisical wilderness as you could find anywhere in America. Countless millions of waterbirds inhabited the Everglades—roseate spoonbills, white ibises, storks, herons, great rafts of migrating ducks on the ponds, and large flocks of flamingos that flew in from the Bahamas. Primitive man wanted for nothing.

In the late winter, after the water retreated to ponds and canoe trails, the resident Indians set fire to the sawgrass. These fires served a purpose. They burned everything down to the moist black muck in which the sawgrass grew and kept the glades open by preventing encroachment of trees. After the Everglades were drained the fires did not stop at the soil surface, but burned deeply into the dry muck. Fire also invaded the tree islands, dried out by drainage, burning the accumulated leafmold and destroying centuries-old live oaks and other hardwoods. But in 1910, two years before the opening of the drainage canals, the Everglades were much like the ancient Indians had known them. There may not have been as many birds, because the plume hunters had decimated the beautiful winged creatures, but deer were plentiful and there were enough white ibises for anyone handy with a gun to satisfy his taste for curlew. Moreover, the ponds, countless alligator holes, and sloughs were teeming with fish, particularly in the spring when the Ox-Woman began her journey.

We don't know where she began her trip. She probably left from the vicinity of Paradise Key, now the site of the Royal Palm Ranger Station in the Everglades National Park. She had camped at Paradise Key, and one of the oxen she brought from Georgia died there. The other died in a farmer's backyard in south Dade. So she had two young oxen, which she had broken herself, when she started her journey. Leaving from Paradise Key, she would have had to cross only about twenty miles of open glades, including the Shark River Slough which in the dry season held a foot or so of water. But there would have been no deep streams to cross, and cloven-footed oxen could have made it through the deepest muck without bogging down. After crossing the Everglades, the Ox-Woman entered a twenty-mile-wide stretch of pine islands interspersed with glades and thin cypress. But after that she had to cross Big Cypress Swamp, with its dense cypress strands between open glades. There may have been times when the Ox-Woman had to chop her way for long distances, but she was handy with an ax and this would have been no undue hardship. But wide Indian trails crossed the cypress strands long before the white man came; and after the earliest pioneers arrived they explored much of the cypress, always looking for greener pastures beyond. So the Ox-Woman might have been able to follow old wagon roads through the swamps north of Turner River. Although she could have had no accurate charts, she undoubtedly had talked to local Crackers, hunters, and possibly to Seminole Indians who knew this country.

Whatever route Mrs. McLain chose, it must have taken her four to six weeks. But she would have had plenty to eat and, after crossing the open glades, there was grass for the oxen. In Big Cypress Swamp she could have added wild turkey and fox squirrel to her own diet. But wouldn't a woman, never sure exactly where she was and having no idea when she would reach her destination, have been scared of the boogery swamp? What about the panthers, bears, snakes, and alligators? Mrs. McLain must have been well acquainted with these animals and reptiles long before she came to Florida, since she was reared on the edge of the Okefenokee Swamp in Georgia. She had her dogs with her to bark off camp invaders at night, and she must have kept a campfire going. And, of course, she had her shotgun.

Reaching Everglades, the Ox-Woman found her sister, Hannah, or "Big Six," as the local people had nicknamed her. She was earning a living cutting buttonwood for the making of charcoal. This life did not suit the older sister, however, and, finding no land suitable for farming, Mrs. McLain remained at Everglades only a few weeks. But she made no attempt to retrace her trail across the glades and swamps. Instead, she set out for Immokalee, thirty-five miles north. Several miles east of Immokalee she found an Indian mound, of about ten acres in size, along the edge of a cypress swamp. Here the big woman built herself a palmetto shack, near a canoe landing used by pre-Colombian Indians.

On June 12, 1911, *The Miami Metropolis,* now *The Miami News,* carried an announcement of Mrs. Sarah McLain's death. She was reported slain by a man to whose house she had gone to collect a debt. The story recounted that she and her oxen had been a familiar sight in Dade County for several years. The story made no mention of her trip across the Everglades. However, two poets in south Dade who had known the Ox-Woman were inspired to memorialize her trip in verse. Lilly Lawrence Bow wrote:

"She drove her oxen
    Across the glade
Urged by the sound of the
    Panther's wail
Where no man had walked
    She blazed a trail."

Annie May Fitzpatrick wrote that the Ox-Woman
"Crossed the glades with her
    little ox team,
Not for glory or gain but
    to sustain
Her faith in her wanderlust
    dream."

Neither Mrs. Bow nor Mrs. Fitzpatrick may ever have

learned that the story in the *Metropolis* was incorrect. It was
Hannah Smith, and not the Ox-Woman, who was slain. Not
just one but five persons died, and the murders had to be
written off as unsolved crimes because the accused and only
surviving witness was himself slain.

Shortly after her sister departed, Big Six went to work for
Ed Watson, who had a sugarcane farm and syrup factory at
Chatham Bend in the Ten Thousand Island, twenty miles
south of Chokoloskee Island. Two men were hired along with
her, Dutchy Melvin, a fugitive from justice at Key West, and a
man with a questionable past named Waller. Their job was to
cut firewood for the syrup boiler and to harvest sugarcane. In
middle October, 1910, a clam fisherman named Cannon and
his small son were going up the Chatham River when the boy
spotted a huge foot sticking out of the water. But the father,
nearsighted, pooh-poohed his son for imagining things. When
the Cannons returned later, the body to which the foot belonged had risen partly out of the water. Cannon recognized
the body as that of Hannah Smith. Nearby, in a shoal area,
the Cannons spotted two other bodies. Putting his motor of
his boat in high gear, Cannon headed for Pavilion Key, a
clam-fishing center six miles away, and spread the alarm.

Today this area of the Ten Thousand Islands is part of the
Everglades National Park. The clam fishing disappeared long
ago, the heavy dredging having destroyed the clams. The Watson house has disappeared, too, but the syrup boiler is still
there, and so is a gnarled old royal poinciana tree which puts
on a show of crimson color in early summer.

The Cannons' discovery created a charged atmosphere in
the fishing camp. Ed Watson, who had a reputation as a
killer, was both hated and feared. He was over six feet, wore
a black handlebar mustache, and carried a six-shooter in his
belt. In his boat he always carried a shotgun. A native of
Lake City, in north Florida, Watson had fled to Oklahoma
Territory in the 1880s after slaying a couple of cousins with

whom he had argued. He became a confererate of the famous
woman outlaw, Belle Starr. He bragged in Smallwood's store,
which still stands on Chokoloskee Island, that he had accompanied the outlaw and her gang on several train robberies. He
also claimed that he had slain Belle Starr, "because she
crossed me up." Watson fled to the Ten Thousand Islands
after the ambush slaying and settled with his wife and three
children at Chatham Bend, where he built a house and
planted sugarcane. He later built a home in Fort Myers,
where his family lived while the children were in school.
Living on the farm permanently was a foreman, Leslie Cox.

Upon hearing of the three deaths at Chatham Bend, the
fishermen at Pavilion Key had no doubt that Watson was the
slayer. Chatham Bend was in Monroe County and the sheriff
was at Key West. It would take three or four days, perhaps
longer, to go get him. Furthermore, the weather was squally
and the barometer was dropping. It appeared that a hurricane
was coming. So the fishermen got their guns and took to
their boats to call on Watson. They knew there would be no
rest in the Ten Thousand Islands so long as a killer was at
large. But when confronted by the angry fishermen, Watson
denied having anything to do with the slayings.

"Well, who did?" demanded a fisherman.

"Cox," replied Watson. "Leslie Cox, my foreman, did the
killings."

"Where is he?"

"He ain't here now," replied Watson, "but I expect him in
later."

"Well, when he comes in," said Henry Short, a rough-
skinned fisherman, "bring him to Chokoloskee, dead or
alive."

The fishermen departed, to bury the bodies before returning to camp. Meanwhile, the squalls had grown stronger and
more frequent. In the night a hurricane hit, the most severe
to hit Florida in the early part of this century. A six-foot tide

covered most of the islands. The only ones escaping the flood were those in which Indians had built kitchen middens, as at Chatham Bend and Chokoloskee. It was two days before the fishermen could leave Pavilion Key and go to Chokoloskee. There they found other fishermen gathered about Smallwood's Store. Everyone was armed. Later in the day Watson arrived in a motorized skiff, alone, and came ashore near the store. Here he was met by a "committee of two," Henry Short and Harry Brown, appointed by the fishermen to "do the talking." Meanwhile, the others stood nearby, armed, silent, and tense.

"Where's Cox?"asked Short.

"I don't have Cox; I shot him and he fell overboard," replied Watson, reaching into the boat, "but I brought his hat."

Whereupon Watson tossed a straw hat onto the shore and came up with a double-barrel shotgun. Did he intend to use the shotgun or did he intend only to bring it ashore? Nobody will ever know. Immediately the fishermen raised pistols, rifles, and shotguns and began firing. Watson collapsed in his boat and died.

The body was taken to Rabbit Key, on the edge of the Gulf, and buried. Later Watson's son-in-law had the bones exhumed and buried in the Fort Myers City Cemetery. The body of Cox was never found, while the bones of Big Six, Waller, and Melvin lie in unmarked graves at Chatham River.

The motive for the slayings will never be known. Many guesses have been made. The persistent theory is that Watson owed these people wages for several weeks of work, and figured it was cheaper to pay off in lead than in cash. On the other hand, Watson may have told the fishermen the truth. Cox may have shot the three after an argument. Maybe Watson had to shoot Cox in self-defense.

And what happened to the Ox-Woman? About 1915 she pulled up stakes at her Indian mound farm near Immokalee and moved to a site near Fort Denaud, north of the Caloosahatchee River. In 1919 she died after suffering a stroke and was buried in the Fort Denaud Cemetery.

THIRTEEN

The Wizard's Ghost

Early in 1885 Thomas A. Edison took the first vacation of his life. He had been in declining health since his invention of the electric light in 1879, on which he had worked night and day for several years. The frustrations in building the first electric power distribution system, which he completed in New York in 1882, had done nothing to aid his health. Then, in 1884, he lost his wife, Mary Stilwell. Leaving his laboratory at Menlo Park, New Jersey, he came to the Saint Johns River, staying a short time before going on to Saint Augustine.

Had the winter been normal, with the usual number of sunny days, Edison probably would have stayed out his vacation in the Oldest City. But January and February had been both cold and wet, and when Edison was given a chance to go to Fort Myers on board a small yacht, he decided to leave

BobLamme

dreary Saint Augustine. He remained in Fort Myers for several weeks, and when time came for him to return to Menlo Park he had purchased fourteen acres on the Caloosahatchee River, a quarter-mile from town. He wasted no time in drawing plans for two identical houses, to be connected by a breezeway, and had them prefabricated in Fairfield, Maine, in the winter of 1885-86. That spring the sections were transported by schooner to Fort Myers and put together. These identical two-story houses stand today exactly as they were when Edison brought his second wife to Fort Myers in 1886. One house was to serve as the Edisons' home, the other as a guest house. Nearby Edison built a small laboratory. He would build a larger one later. Over the spacious grounds Edison planted rare tropical trees that his friends sent him. And here he lived and worked every winter until his death in 1931 at eighty-four.

Mrs. Edison gave the estate to the city of Fort Myers before her death in 1947, and today it is operated as a museum and botanical garden. A small admission is charged to provide funds for maintenance. In my travels through Florida I have yet to find a more inspiring attraction. I had the pleasure of touring the estate with Curator Robert C. Halgrim, who, as a young man, worked for Edison. Halgrim not only has an intimate knowledge of the place—the houses, the laboratory, the trees and the estate's history—but he possesses recollections of the great inventor and colorful personality that help to make the place come to life as you walk through it.

Everything is much the same as the "Wizard of Menlo Park" left it forty years ago. Edison's old rubber gloves, which he used while mixing chemicals, hang rotting in the laboratory where he put them. And in the office is the cot where he used to break his long days with fifteen-minute naps. You study the cot, the desk, the numerous mementos and inventions, the green curtains drawn halfway down the broad windows, and you have the feeling that the Wizard may pop in any moment and be surprised to find a stranger in his office.

"Mr. Edison used to say that because he was deaf he could get more rest in fifteen minutes than most persons could get in hours," said Halgrim. "Nothing disturbed him. His deafness also helped him to concentrate."

Edison was not stone deaf; he was just hard of hearing. Able to read lips, he could "listen" to others talk far beyond the distance that a person of normal hearing could. Halgrim recalled the time Edison happened to be looking when a new employee made a dirty remark.

" 'Fire that man,' Mr. Edison said. None of the rest of us had heard the man; he was too far away and had spoken just above a whisper to a fellow worker," Halgrim remembered. "But the man was let go. Mr. Edison wouldn't tolerate dirty talk among his employees."

Halgrim has turned aside suggestions that he remove the dust and polish the laboratory equipment.

"Too many hazards are involved," he said. "First, there are the chances of breakage, and, second, the arrangements soon would be changed. It wouldn't take many years to destroy surfaces. We think it's better to leave everything just as it is, with the dust and all."

In Edison's later years he studied the goldenrod plant as a source of rubber, and much of the chemical apparatus in the laboratory reflects his interest in this project. He collected and grew countless species and varieties of goldenrod in Florida, cross-breeding them in an effort to produce a plant that would yield latex in commercial quantities. Firestone and Ford financed the project. Edison's aim was to make it possible for the United States to become an independent producer of rubber in wartime. Although unsuccessful, Edison began the research that led eventually to the development of synthetic rubber.

Throughout the laboratory and office are mementos of Edison's famous inventions—the electric light, phonograph, movie projector, and Edison-Bell telephone. Although Alexander Graham Bell invented the telephone, in 1876, he soon lost interest in it. Edison perfected the telephone and his company made component parts for it. Edison also set up a transmission system capable of carrying more than one conversation at a time.

A tour of the estate, including the laboratory, the residence, the botanical garden, and a new museum take about an hour. Many visitors enjoy the residence and the grounds as much as the laboratory, because they are more understandable. The identical houses are connected by covered colonnade with a tile walk. The living rooms of the houses are lighted by bulbs which were among the first incadescent lights Edison manufactured. Impressively, they still burn fourteen hours a day although more than half a century old, which tells us something about today's electric light bulb that usually lasts but a few hundred hours.

Edison, according to Halgrim, built his residence and guest house exactly alike because he wanted guests to feel that. they were being treated equally to their hosts.

"Whenever Mr. Edison visited someone, he didn't like to be shunted away in a tiny guest cottage," said Halgrim, "and he wouldn't do a guest like that himself. Mr. Edison was an extremely sensitive individual, and if he was concerned about his own feelings he was equally concerned about the feelings of others."

Among his more notable guests were John Burroughs, Harvey Firestone, and Henry Ford. Ford in 1916 purchased adjoining property and spent a part of each winter in Fort Myers until after Edison's death. Whenever his three famous friends were in town, Edison would take time off from his laboratory to accompany them about the countryside. They liked to go up the Caloosahatchee River, where Ford had a plantation near LaBelle. That was before the winding, picturesque river was reduced to a straight ditch by the Corps of Engineers to facilitate the runoff of flood water from Lake Okeechobee. They also liked to drive to Estero, twelve miles south of Fort Myers, to visit Koreshan Unity's botanical garden and to sample the unusual tropical fruits in season and the jams and jellies made from these fruits. On one occasion the three made a tour deep into Big Cypress Swamp, returning with quantities of wild orchids, which were planted in trees in Edison's garden. Some of these orchids have survived half a century.

On the second floor of his residence Edison had a hideaway where he could go off by himself to relax and read.

"He jokingly referred to this room as his 'dog house,' " said Halgrim. "He used to say that he retired here after he and Mrs. Edison had a spat. Everyone took such statements with a grain of salt. He and Mrs. Edison may have had their differences, but they got along well."

Edison started his plant collection when he began spending winters in Fort Myers in 1886, and he continued to collect as long as he lived. A rubber tree Firestone brought from India in 1925 as a gift now covers nearly half an acre. One of the most curious trees in the garden is a Morton Bay Fig, a rubber tree from Australia, whose serpentine roots rise high enough above ground to make comfortable seats. There also are many flowering trees, most of which bloom in wintertime or early spring, during the period of Edison's residence in Florida. Edison's plantings did not stop within the walls of his estate. He brought from Cuba the seeds of the Cuban royal palm at about the turn of the century and grew enough of these handsome palms to plant two miles on either side of McGregor Boulevard, which passes by his estate. Edison's avenue of palms was later extended fifteen miles.

At the time I was visiting the estate Halgrim was putting the finishing touches on a museum in ,which many of the early products of Edison's inventions were to be displayed.

Included was the third Model T that Henry Ford built.

"Mr. Edison insisted on driving the Model T even though Mr. Ford offered to give him a new Lincoln to replace it," said Halgrim. "It still runs perfectly," he added as he switched on the ignition and adjusted the spark and gas levers beneath the steering wheel. He pulled up on the crank a couple of times and the old four-cylinder motor started. Halgrim returned to the side of the car to adjust the throttle until the motor was barely turning over, an indication of perfect adjustment of the timing and the spark.

"Listen to it cadillac," he said, using a Model T Ford terminology I hadn't heard since the twenties.

On the car is a set of tires Firestone manufactured from goldenrod rubber Edison extracted in his Fort Myers laboratory, making them one of the most expensive sets of tires in the United States.

Since my visit to the Edison Estate, the inventor's study, in a separate building, has burned. It was a replica of the first laboratory Edison built in 1886. Early in the 1920s, after Edison had built a larger laboratory, Ford persuaded him to give up the old laboratory building to the Ford Museum in Dearborn. The building was moved to Michigan intact, along with the soil from the site for use as the foundation. But Edison missed the old building, where he had received so much inspiration, so his wife secretly had a replica planned. While her husband was out of town for several days in 1925 carpenters erected the building. Upon Edison's return his wife presented him with the building as a birthday gift. He used it as a study. Destroyed in the fire were many books and papers, as well as an enlargement showing Edison with his friends, Burroughs, Firestone, and Ford. Destroyed also was an unusual cross section of Koreshan Unity's concept of the universe, with the sun in the center of a globe and with man living on the inside of a much larger earth. Edison did not believe the Koreshan concept, but he was a tolerant person interested in all varieties of ideas; and he kept the memento by his desk, probably as a reminder of the unusual facility of man's mind.

But just as great a reminder of man's facility to think all kinds of unusual things is the Edison laboratory. Perhaps in our modern day, when discovery and invention are usually the result of teamwork by engineers and Ph.D. level scientists, the dusty old lab may no longer be much of an inspiration to youth. But to those of us who remember when the Wizard was one of the world's most famous men because of his contributions to our personal comforts, as well as to our enjoyment of life, a visit to the Edison place is richly rewarding.

FOURTEEN

Three-Ring Sideshow

The first time I visited the Ringling Museums in Sarasota I made the mistake of going through the Ringling Museum of Art first. I should have gone first through the Museum of the Circus, then through John Ringling's colorful Venetian palace, "Ca' d'Zan," before venturing into the art museum.

This route I recommend to anyone visiting the Ringling Museums, except perhaps the sophisticated art buff. To know something about the circus and about the flamboyant circus king is to add another dimension to your appreciation of the art collection. Most of the paintings are of the Baroque period, to which you are introduced in the enormous and bold canvases by Peter Paul Rubens. And what could be more baroque than the circus, or John Ringling, the fabulous personality who collected the pictures?

BOB LAMME

Ringling, a gargantuan man of gargantuan ideas, was intimately associated with the circus for most of his seventy years, helping his six brothers to build Ringling Bros. and Barnum & Bailey into "The Greatest Show on Earth." From his teens Ringling was as much a part of the circus as the clowns, the acrobats, the animal trainers, and the colorful wagons.

Ringling purchased the sixty-acre site where the museums are located in 1911, but it was not until 1925 that he developed it. First he and his wife Mable built their residence, in the style of a Venetian palace. Then he built a museum, in Italian Renaissance style, to house his collection of art. He left everything to the state of Florida upon his death in 1936. The circus museum was added in 1948. Another gem to be found on a tour of the grounds is the Asolo Theater, built in 1798 in Asolo, Italy, and purchased by the state in 1949.

During tours of Europe in search of talent for his circus, Ringling and his wife took in most of the art museums of the Continent. Gradually they became ardent admirers of European art and architecture. Moreover, Ringling bought and read countless books on the subjects. And, as you might expect of a circus king, his interest gradually became focused on the colorful, ostentatious, curlicued art of the Baroque period.

The Baroque period was to Ringling best exemplified by the buxom Nordic girls painted by Rubens with such splendid candor in the early part of the 1600s. Ringling's taste came naturally. Those girls were much like the figures he was accustomed to see decorate the sides of the circus wagons—bold, extravagant, and flamboyant carvings, painted in gold and red.

During the 1920s Baroque art was about the cheapest art you could buy. It was temporarily out of style. If you had good taste you went in for something more modern, more elegant, more sophisticated. But Ringling didn't care a hang for what others thought of his taste. Going on a buying binge, within two years he had made one of the finest collections of Baroque art outside of Europe. For those four huge Rubens canvases you see upon entering the art museum Ringling paid only $150,000. So large were the canvases that the Duke of Westminster, from whom Ringling purchased them, had no place in his castle to hang them. Neither did Ringling. He brought them to America rolled up and had a special room designed when the architect was drawing up plans for a museum.

The four pictures, which Rubens painted as full scale models for tapestries, are dramatic subjects from the Old Testament, done in such robust design, form, and color that to stand before them in contemplation is a stunning and unforgettable experience. But there are several other Rubens paintings in the long gallery beyond the special room. Ringling had a fondness for the Flemish painter and apparently bought all the paintings by him he found for sale. Before Ringling stopped buying about 1930, he had acquired more than 500 paintings, including many from the Renaissance period. He sometimes had to buy paintings he cared little for in order to acquire paintings that appealed to him. Despite his preference for the Baroque, he wound up with a collection stretching across several centuries. Amazingly, Ringling seldom got stuck with phony art, as so many other wealthy collectors have done. He bought through reputable dealers, but he also had the keen eyes of a circus king.

Ringling's talents as a trader are revealed in the way he acquired the *Portrait of an Unidentified Cardinal* by Sassoferrato, one of the most attractive paintings in the museum. He had all but closed a contract to buy a number of paintings from an European dealer. Pointing to the painting of the cardinal, whose colorful garb appealed to his circus taste, Ringling said:

"Throw in that Sassafras and I'll take the lot."

The dealer "threw" it in. Today it is worth more than $100,000.

The Ringlings began building their Venetian mansion in 1925. It took two years to complete and to furnish. The story goes that Ringling would have been satisfied with a "little bit of a place," but Mable wanted something that would remind her of Venice, a city both had enjoyed so much during their many visits there. Mable had the architect, Dwight James Baum, adapt the facade of the Doge's Palace in Venice and the tower of the old Madison Square Garden, where the Ringlings had seen so many circuses open. The design is a mixture of Gothic and Renaissance, and, although the decorations are ostentatious, the building possesses beauty and a warmth that are lacking in Vizcaya in Miami and Flagler's Whitehall in Palm Beach. The interior is no less striking, the thirty rooms being furnished with furniture that came out of such estates as those of Vincent Astor and Jay Gould. With its art, stained glass windows, tapestries, hand-wrought ironwork, and pecky cypress ceiling in the main hall, the house is one of the most successful of the ostentatious homes built at a time when the rich had to pay but a fraction of the taxes they have to pay today.

At the time Ringling built a museum to house his art collection he was absolute king of the circus and one of the wealthiest men in America. After the death in 1927 of his only living brother, Charles, Ringling transferred the winter quarters of the circus from Bridgeport, Connecticut, to Sarasota. He lost Mable in 1929 and in 1930 married Mrs. Emily Haag Buck. But his bride would not tolerate Ringling's arrogance and eccentricities as the acquiescent Mable had done, and they soon separated. In his will, Ringling cut her off with one dollar.

Ringling changed his will several times, with each subsequent one, or codicil, adding new complications that would haunt his memory long after his death. He left the art museum and the mansion, together with sixty acres of property, to the state of Florida. To the state he also left half the remainder of his estate, for the maintenance of his art collection. The other half he left to his only sister, Mrs. Ida North. He named her and her oldest son, John Ringling North, executors, while her other son, Henry North, was made a trustee. But Ringling fell out with his nephews and changed his will again, adding a codicil that left the bulk of his estate to Florida and provided only $5,000 a year for his sister. In the same will he cut off his nephews, an unnecessary act because they were not beneficiaries anyway. However, Ringling neglected to remove the names of his sister and nephew as executors. Perhaps he thought the wording of the codocil was sufficient to take care of that.

The market crash of 1929 and the depression that followed hit Ringling hard, but after his death his estate was appraised at $23.5 million. A ten-year court battle over the estate followed, waged by Ringling's relatives and his widow, the former Mrs. Buck. It was not until 1947 that Florida took over the museum and mansion, settling its claim against the estate for $1 million. John Ringling North, cut out of his uncle's will, actually became one of the chief beneficiaries, winding up with $1 million, the fee for his services as executor.

The art collection was in 1947 appraised at $15 million, but today its value is incalculable. The many Rubens canvases alone probably would bring more than the value of the entire collection in 1947. And add to these the value of precious works by Rembrandt, Velasquez, Murillo, El Greco, Ribera, Sassoferrato, Bassano, Dolci, and Veronese, plus the sculptures and the bronze copies of Greek, Roman, and Renaissance sculpture that decorate the museum grounds. Dolci's *Blue Madonna* is one of the most striking madonnas in the world, while the dead figure in Rembrandt's *Lamentation*

Over the Dead Christ is done in such realism that as you
stand before it you know the artist had to use a cadaver as a
model. The deep and touching sympathy on the faces of the
onlookers, emerging from the darkness against the background of the cross—and particularly the disconsolate expression of a boy leaning against the cross as he views the dead
Christ—make this one of the most moving Rembrandts I have
ever seen.

The Museum of the Circus brought criticism from local
cultural buffs when it was established in 1948. Fortunately,
the cultural buffs were overridden, and today the circus museum holds a valuable and fascinating collection of circus
paraphernalia from a period that will not exist again. Among
the museum's circus wagons are the famous Barnum & Bailey
forty-horse bandwagon, "Five Graces," built in 1878; the
"Bell Wagon," used in Ringling Bros. circus parades, and
Sells-Floto Circus' "The Two Jesters" calliope wagon, containing one of the largest steam calliopes ever made.

After you study the decorative carvings done for these
wagons by unnamed sculptors, nobody will have to suggest to
you the relationship between the circus and John Ringling's
love for Baroque art. One is just as Baroque as the other.

FIFTEEN

Out of the Arabian Nights

✑

As examples of extravagance and luxury, Saint Augustine has its Ponce de Leon Hotel, Palm Beach has its Whitehall, and Miami has its Vizcaya, but for the bizarre no other city in Florida—and few in America—can match the Tampa Bay Hotel. This sprawling brick structure, with its Moorish arches supporting wide porches and topped with thirteen Moslem-like minarets, looks like something out of the Arabian Nights.

Now the home of the University of Tampa, the 511-room hotel was begun in 1888 by Henry B. Plant, railroad king, the year Henry M. Flagler opened his Ponce de Leon Hotel. Plant, a Connecticut Yankee, came to Georgia after the Civil War and made a fortune out of the railway express business. During a period of major depression between 1873 and 1879 Plant bought several bankrupt railroads for "peanuts" and, by 1884, owned a network connecting Savannah, Jacksonville, and Tampa. Upon seeing Flagler build a luxury hotel at Saint Augustine, Plant wasn't going to be outdone. His answer was the luxurious, ostentatious, and bizarre Tampa Bay Hotel.

Plant set his hotel behind the largest live oak in the area, the DeSoto Oak on Hillsborough River, so named because of a tradition that Hernando DeSoto bargained with the Indians here upon his landing in 1539. The oak, its branches casting a shadow 120 feet across, probably was standing when DeSoto landed, but there is no evidence the the conquistador saw the tree. The oak is worthwhile to see even without the added attraction of the eighty-year-old hotel.

When Plant opened the hotel in 1891 it covered six acres, while its walls contained 452 railroad carloads of brick—more than ten trainloads at forty cars to the train. Plant believed he had built the most magnificent hotel in the world. Certainly the architecture was among the most unusual in the world outside of Mecca or Granada. The structure had been patterned after the Alhambra, with Mecca overtones. The hotel cost Plant a fortune in eighteen-nineties money—$3 million to build and more than $1 million to furnish. He and Mrs. Plant made a round-the-world cruise to buy furniture and decorations. The furniture was said to have been owned by the rulers of Europe, Marie Antoinette, Louis XIV, and Napoleon. From the Orient they brought back wood carvings and huge urns which they figured would fit well in the Moorish atmosphere.

In 1891 some 7,000 persons lived in Tampa. Most of the residents wouldn't have had enough money to buy a shot of whiskey at the hotel's bar. Nor was Tampa a tourist town as was Saint Augustine where Flagler had built the Ponce de Leon Hotel. So Plant had to spend thousands of dollars in promotion and in the entertainment of celebrities as a means of enticing wealthy paying guests. Plant mailed 15,000 invitations to the opening. The hotel was filled, and, according to

The Tampa Tribune, the opening night was one that would "long be remembered."

Opening in early February and closing in April, during this short period the hotel entertained 4,367 guests. How many paid we don't know. But if Plant failed to make a profit, the community enjoyed a new kind of prosperity, and, according to the *Tribune,* a gala occasion. The "gala occasion" occurred every winter while the hotel was open. The biggest was in 1895 when a travel agency brought Mrs. Ulysses S. Grant to Tampa. All of Tampa celebrated, with a parade and dances in the evenings.

Plant appears to have been one of the first hotel owners to make an effort to attract conventions, among which was the National Fish Congress. But before the hotel could develop its full potentials as a convention center, the Spanish-American War started and the Army took over the hotel. Colonel Theodore Roosevelt trained his brown-clad Rough Riders on the hotel grounds. He stayed in camp with his men, but Mrs. Roosevelt stayed at the hotel. War correspondents Richard Harding Davis and Stephen Crane rocked on the porches behind the Moorish arches, along with the military and their wives, whenever they were not in the bar.

Plant died in 1899 at the age of eighty-four, and his heirs could hardly wait to dispose of the Arabian Nights white elephant. Unable to find a sucker, they finally traded the hotel in 1905 to the city of Tampa in exchange for a settlement of taxes and $125,000. For a time the city tried its hand at hotel operation, but as in so many other instances when government gets involved in business, the venture proved costly. Tampa never was an important tourist town, despite Plant's efforts to make it one. Moreover, two years before his death Plant had opened the Belleview Biltmore near Clearwater. With its two golf courses and its nearness to the Gulf beaches, the newer hotel was an immediate success, so much so that major additions were necessary after Plant's death.

For years Tampa sought to sell its Moorish ghost, for almost any price, in order to get the property back on the tax roll. The city never did get the hotel back on the tax roll, but did the next best thing: it leased the structure to the two-year-old University of Tampa in 1933 for ninety-nine years at a dollar a year. The city retained a portion of the first floor, which was converted into the Tampa Municipal Museum. Here are many of the furnishings the Plants purchased for the hotel. Some of them might be described as "out of this world." They represent the extravagant taste that existed among wealthy Americans as the nineteenth century was ending, when this country was beginning to sense its weight and feel its affluence in the world—except in its taste.

Even in its dollar-a-year quarters the University of Tampa had no easy time. It was founded at the beginning of a long depression which was followed by World War II. When the state-owned University of South Florida was founded at Tampa in 1956 it looked like the end for the privately owned university. But David Delo, the president, told worried trustees he though the competition would be good for the small institution.

"A little competition never hurt anyone," he said.

He was right. The university not only survived in competition with a major state institution having a student body of more than 15,000, but has made considerable progress. In fact, the University of Tampa grew so fast that new dormitories and classroom buildings had to be added. The student body doubled, from about a thousand to more than 2,000. Moreover, the old grads began aiding their alma mater. It's most certainly the kind of university a student could never forget. And neither could a visitor, even if the visitor stayed but an hour instead of four years.

SIXTEEN

Tower on the Ridge

To Edward W. Bok, a shy, introspective, foreign-born publisher and onetime editor of *The Ladies Home Journal* must go the credit for creating Florida's first major man-made tourist attraction—Mountain Lake Sanctuary and the Singing Tower, four miles northeast of Lake Wales. Standing atop a 294-foot hill called Iron Mountain, highest point in central Florida, the tower can be seen for miles around. Millions have come to see it since its completion in 1928—to stroll through the magnificent gardens about the base of the tower and to hear the carillon concerts.

In 1929, when Calvin Coolidge came down to dedicate Bok's tower and gardens, 70,000 poured into Lake Wales to hear the president, who was winding up his second term. From then on tourists came in increasing numbers until half a million were coming each year. The tower and the gardens

BOB LAMME

proved to be the capping achievement of Bok's life. He died
in 1930 at the age of sixty-seven without realizing what a
boon he had created.

A Dutch boy who made good in America through sheer
devotion to industry, Bok became a millionaire in the publishing business. In 1915, shortly before his retirement, Bok
came to Lake Wales to visit friends living in exclusive Mountain Lakes Estates, a 3,500-acre millionaires' winter hideaway
which had been planned by America's most famous landscape
architectural firm, Olmsted Bros. of Brookline, Massachusetts. Frederick S. Ruth of Baltimore, founder of the estates, offered rich northern residents a unique opportunity.
They could own a winter home in a beautiful setting of rolling countryside about Mountain Lake, at the foot of Iron
Mountain, and also own a citrus grove, with the company
managing the grove and selling the fruit. Ruth's prospectus,
suggesting that the grove would pay the cost of maintaining a
winter home in Florida, evidently appealed to the thrifty
rich.

Bok was so impressed by Mountain Lake that upon his
retirement in the early twenties he bought a home at the foot
of dome-shaped Iron Mountain, which stood near the center
of the five-square mile home and grove development. From
Bok's dooryard he could look up at the hill behind the home,
which was impressive despite the water tower that occupied
its summit. On pleasantly cool but sunshiny days, so common to central Florida during the winter, Bok would frequently follow a trail to the top of the hill and stroll through
the pines and saw palmettos which covered the dome. He
liked particularly to view sunsets from the summit. The
woods atop Iron Mountain became a sort of sanctuary for the
comtemplative Bok. Here it was quiet, with only the sounds
of birds to break the silence, or perhaps the soughing of the
wind through the pines. During these periods of walking and
contemplation an idea began to grow in his mind. Why not

create a garden here, to be dedicated as a sanctuary for man
and for the wild things seeking haven from the often oppres-
sive outside world?

Bok went to Ruth and told him of his plan, and asked the
developer to sell him the summit of Iron Mountain. The practical Ruth wasted no time in accepting Bok's offer, because
to him the summit of Iron Mountain was useless, being un-
suited either as a site for homes or for citrus. Bok then
brought in Frederick Law Olmsted, Jr., landscape architect,
and walked over the dome with him, at the same time describing his dreams of creating here a sanctuary for man and
birds. Olmsted was a highly perceptive, sensitive person, re-
puted to be at least as able as his father, who had designed
New York City's Central Park and the gardens of the Vanderbilt estate at Biltmore, North Carolina. Olmsted went to
work on a plan, and, upon its approval by Bok, the laborious
task of clearing the palmettos, creating trails, and the planting of trees and shrubbery was begun. In charge of the task
force was William Lyman Phillips, formerly a student of Olmsted at Harvard, who had laid out the town of Balboa in the
Canal Zone and had recently returned from France where he
had assisted in designing the landscape planting about America's World War I cemeteries. Phillips was to remain in Florida
for the rest of his life, to plan the public parks of Dade
County and to design the Fairchild Tropical Garden, his outstanding achievement.

Bok watched the progress of his sanctuary gardens with
utmost satisfaction. Phillips scouted Florida in search of suitable plants; not particularly showy ones, but plants that produced food and shelter for birds. The gardens took more than
two years to complete. They turned out to be as Bok had
dreamed, a quiet and inspiring sanctuary. He enjoyed walking
along the trails, stopping to watch the birds which were now
beginning to use the dense foliage planted especially for
them. Such satisfaction did the gardens give him that Bok

invited his neighbors to enjoy the secluded spot. And then he began to invite persons he met outside of Mountain Lake Estates, particularly in Lake Wales.

Visitors coming from outside the guarded entrance to Mountain Lake were advised to take a separate road which took them to the top of the mountain from a side entrance. More and more people learned of the winding, dirt road that led to Bok's gardens, and visits by outsiders increased, as much out of sheer curiosity as of enjoyment of the unique sanctuary. If the wealthy residents at the foot of the hill were displeased they made no great objection, because they never themselves saw the visitors, and in time Mountain Lake Sanctuary, as Bok called his gardens, became known far and wide in central Florida as a place where everyone was invited.

Bok was pleased to have others share his delights. But as time passed the garden became less pleasing to him, not because anything was wrong with the design or the planting. Olmsted and Phillips had done a marvelous job of creating the kind of sanctuary the contemplative, sometimes brooding, Dutchman had conceived. Yet, something was missing. The gardens needed a central focal point, something striking and beautiful on which the eyes could dwell when one strolled to the end of a vista and turned around. Bok now would stroll through the vistas and look for that focal point, but only the ugly water tower caught his eyes. Day after day, upon his visits to the sanctuary, this problem occupied his mind. That water tower and its ugliness could not be erased. It stood there upon the crest of the dome, dominating the view from every direction.

Bok had seen at Malines, Belgium, a famous belltower that likewise dominated the landscape because it, too, was a principal focal point. But it was a beautiful thing. And then there were the wonderful sounds emitted by its great bells. One could not help pausing to look up at the tower when those bells clanged. Bok found himself picturing the Malines belltower in the center of Mountain Lake Sanctuary; and so impressed was he that the tower image refused to leave his mind. There were times, while he paused to look up at the imaginary tower, he envisioned the sounds of a carillon which he was beginning to include in his image. One day shortly after 1925 Bok made a decision. He would build such a tower containing a great carillon, and a reflecting pool. And with this vision, of a tower rising above his garden, its stately shaft reflecting in a quiet pool, he went to Ruth.

Ruth, a businessman and a promoter, had seen how Bok's hilltop gardens had attracted numbers of visitors. A tower such as Bok envisioned would bring even greater numbers. People would flock from great distances to hear the carillon concerts Bok promised to present on special occasions. So Ruth found himself going along with Bok's idea. But the ugly water tower would have to go. An agreement was worked out. Bok would pay for having the tower dismantled and a lower reservoir installed. He was in a hurry. In his brooding way he had a premonition of death, and he wanted the tower completed before the end came.

Built by a Philadelphia firm at an unannounced cost, the tower was completed in late 1928. Near the top of the 205-foot shaft was installed a carillon of seventy-one bells, weighing from eleven pounds to eleven tons. And in the meantime Olmsted Bros. had designed and completed a long reflecting pool at the base of the tower, covering the bottom with concrete to make the basin watertight.

In early 1929, when 70,000 sought to scale Iron Mountain to hear President Coolidge dedicate the Singing Tower, as it had become known, Mountain Lake residents thought they'd "had" it. But the tower and the sanctuary were already there atop the mountain, and all Bok's millionaire neighbors could do was to insist that the curious be kept at a safe distance. So, today 99.99 percent of the tourists who visit Bok's creations are unaware of the estates of the wealthy residents nearby.

For many years it cost nothing to visit the tower. Bok set up a foundation to provide funds for the upkeep of the grounds and to pay the salary of Anton Brees, Belgian carillonneur whom Bok had employed. But the road was poor, and during dry periods a car could get stuck in the deep sand. Having no premonition of the large crowds the tower would attract, Bok had not even provided for a permanent entrance beyond a gentleman's agreement with Ruth. On special days, such as Easter morning, strings of hundreds of automobiles sought to reach the small parking lot beside the sanctuary. As many as 5,000 would attend Easter sunrise services and stand in quiet awe while Brees' carillon rang out as the sun rose from the distant horizon. The aged Brees died several years ago, to be succeeded by younger carillonneurs.

Today a wide, paved highway takes you through the extensive citrus groves of the Mountain Lake Corporation to a spacious, paved parking lot. The road and the lot were built by the corporation, and a guard at the entrance collects a fee from each car to pay for the construction and upkeep. The corporation also operates a gift shop and restaurant in a building just outside the sanctuary grounds.

Bok's premonition of death proved to be well grounded; he lived but a year after the dedication of his sanctuary. While he left funds for perpetual maintenance, he provided nothing for promotion or advertising. So, today it is the town of Lake Wales as well as motels and local tourist attractions that promote the Singing Tower in an effort to keep the tourists coming. Every brochure advertising Lake Wales is sure to include a color photograph of the tower. So popular did the tower become in the thirties that Dick Pope, who created Cypress Gardens, promoted his attraction as being "near the Singing Tower."

Pope no longer mentions the Singing Tower in the extensive promotion literature he circulates every year. He doesn't need to. His colorful gardens, together with professional water ski shows and attractive hostesses dressed like Southern belles of a bygone era, attract more visitors in one day than the Singing Tower and its quiet, colorless gardens draw in a week. This doesn't mean the sanctuary has lost its appeal. But the quiet gardens and tower are more attractive to middle-aged and older people than to younger people looking for more exciting things to do. Upon his death Bok was buried at the foot of the tower. Under his direction something beautiful and pleasing was created—for people, for birds and for the abundant squirrels.

SEVENTEEN

Descendant of the Harem

⚇

The road to Homosassa winds through a hammocklike setting of cabbage palms and old oaks gray with Spanish moss. As you enter the outskirts of the little Gulf Coast community, cottage roof lines begin to appear among the trees. On a hot day you have the feeling the cottages are snuggling to the shade.

Then, just as you have finished rounding a bend, straight ahead is a massive, twenty-foot chimney, constructed of native·limestone. You see at once that the chimney is old; you know it was built long before any of the cottages standing nearby. It is an altogether incongruous object in the landscape. As you approach you see an old-time steam engine flywheel, as well as rust-eaten open boilers, one of which is held within the grasp of gnarled, fingerlike roots of a red cedar tree.

Beside the road near this relic is a parking lot, and you pull in and stop. Beyond the parking area are several picnic tables shaded by live oaks. But nobody is to be seen, not even a caretaker, because it is late in the day, and summer. Big, black mosquitos sing lazily near your ears. A sign tells you this is a Florida State Park and identifies the relic as the Yulee Sugar Mill built in the early 1850s by David L. (L. for Levy) Yulee. Hereabout Yulee owned a 5,000-acre plantation he operated with the help of slaves and which he called by the beautiful name Margarita, the Spanish word for pearl.

One may stroll beneath the oaks, palms, redbays, and cedars, and, while slapping at a mosquito now and then, admire this well-preserved relic of a past era. But nothing about it can match the story of its owner, Florida's first U.S. Senator, David L. Yulee, whose career and background are too improbable for fiction.

Yulee was Florida's first railroad magnate and one of its first millionaires. He built Florida's first cross-state railroad, from Fernandina to Cedar Key, between 1854 and 1860. For a time he was one of Florida's most influential men, being able to borrow money from Yankee bankers at a time when the fate of the Union was in doubt. Only a very poor photograph of David Yulee has been turned up; but according to all reports he possessed a personality so magnetic that his handshake was enough to cut the red tape of Washington bureaucracy or con the most conservative banker into handing him a blank check.

Yulee's father, Moses, was born in a Moroccan harem—the son of the beautiful Rachel Levy, daughter of a Jewish physician of England, and Jacoub ben Youli, grand vizier to the Sultan of Morocco. Rachel was on an English ship, on her way to the British West Indies, when captured by Barbary pirates. The more affluent passengers were held for ransom, the less affluent ones sold into slavery. But Rachel, a young virgin, was a special prize. Taken to Fez under protective guard, Rachel was turned over to the wives of the pirates, who groomed her with great care. Then she was taken to the slave market, stripped, and put on the block with other young virgins. A eunuch of the grand vizier, with a trained eye on Rachel's charms, made the highest bid—and Rachel was delivered to Grand Vizier Youli's harem.

Rachel bore Youli a son, whom she named Moses, and was carrying a second child when the Sultan of Morocco was overthrown, the grand vizier along with him. The harem girls scattered and the pregnant Rachel took her small son to Gibraltar where she soon gave birth to a daughter. She gave both children her family name, Levy.

Moses grew up, bright and sharp-witted, but carrying the mental burden of having been born in a Mohammedan harem. Reaching manhood, the young Jew took his mother and sister to Saint Thomas, in the Virgin Islands, where he went into business. His business thrived, and he married Hannah Abendanone, whose Moorish-Jewish forefathers had been driven from Spain by Ferdinand and Isabella. In 1810 Hannah gave birth to a son, who was named David.

Like the biblical hero for whom he was named, young David was bright and challenging—too much so to remain in the then backward Virgin Islands. So when he was nine his parents sent him to Virginia for his education, while Moses and Hannah moved to Florida where Moses had obtained from Spain a grant of several hundred acres of land in what is now part of the Ocala National Forest.

David, meanwhile, progressed rapidly. Upon finishing school, he soon discovered that his charms and his wit unlocked doors, hearts, and purses. Florida was now a United States possession, and land could be purchased for a dollar an acre. Young David turned on his charms, borrowed thousands of dollars, and acquired thousands of acres of land, eventually becoming wealthy in plantations alone. And he progressed so well in the political arena that when he was only twenty-eight, he became a member of Florida's first constitutional convention, held at old Saint Joseph in 1838. In 1841 he was elected territorial delegate to the U.S. Congress. Then, in 1845 after Florida was admitted to the Union, David was elected to the United States Senate.

Because of some unknown whim, after his election to the Senate, he got the Florida Legislature to pass an act changing his name from David Levy to David L. Yulee, after his Moorish grandfather, Youli. David obviously did not feel there was any particular curse in having a grand vizier for a grandsire, even if he was a Mohammedan. Or, perhaps, he wanted to shed his Hebrew connections. A short time later he married the daughter of Governor Charles Wickliffe of Kentucky, a Protestant.

In the meantime, Senator Yulee was developing a 5,000-acre plantation on the spring-fed Homosassa River, producing mainly sugar but some cotton also, as well as corn and other feed crops for his growing number of cattle. He built a mansion facing the crystal-clear river, and a sugar mill. Here, whenever he could find the time to be at home, he lived like any other Southern aristocrat under a slave economy.

Yulee sided with the South during the Civil War. It has been said that he was one of those who encouraged the war, in order to get out of paying off the huge debt he had incurred in connection with his railroad building. Union soldiers went up the Homosassa River during the war and burned Yulee's mansion, but for some reason failed to set fire to the sugar mill. Perhaps the Union officers felt they could maintain control of the area and enjoy the production of the plantation and mill. Upon the war's end Yulee was arrested by Federal troops on charges he aided the members of Confederate President Jefferson Davis' cabinet in their escape through Florida. He was imprisoned at Fort Pulaski, Georgia, where he remained until President Ulysses S. Grant interceded with a pardon.

Having lost his Florida holdings to creditors, Yulee moved to Washington to live with a married daughter. His name was about forgotten by the time of his death in New York in 1886. But not quite. In Florida a town, Yulee, bore his name, as did a county, Levy.

To leave a community and a county named in one's honor is quite an accomplishment, especially for the grandson of a Moroccan grand vizier, in whose harem his father had been born.

EIGHTEEN

Cross Creek

At Micanopy, ten miles south of Gainesville, you leave U.S. Highway 441 and take a blacktopped road through a mixed countryside of pinewoods, cattle ranches, and little farms. Most of the houses are humble. Some are no more than shanties, standing empty among sagging barns, rotting chicken houses and pig pens—relics of an impoverished agricultural period of Florida's past. After you have driven about six miles the road bends through a setting of moss-draped live-oaks, glossy-leaved magnolias, and tall cabbage palms, and you come to a bridge over a quiet, black stream, its banks lined with the swollen buttresses of cypresses.

This is Cross Creek, a stream a few yards wide connecting Lochloosa Lake and Orange Lake. The creek is only half a mile long. On either side are fishing camps, where you can rent a skiff to go bass or bream fishing or to go duck hunting

BOB LAMME

in season. And you would have no reason to come to Cross Creek except to fish or to hunt—unless you had read Marjorie Kinnan Rawlings' *Cross Creek,* a best seller after its publication by Scribner's in 1942. But no matter what brings you here you are impressed by the primitive charm that must have impressed Mrs. Rawlings when she and her husband, Charles Rawlings, came here to live in the late twenties.

It was my first visit to Cross Creek. As I drove across the bridge, then past house trailers and little cottages where children and dogs played together in the gray, sandy yards, I felt I was being drawn here by much the same curiosity that has attracted many another reader of *Cross Creek* to this little Florida community of the same name. And when I saw gray-haired men and women I wondered if they might have known Mrs. Rawlings, whether perhaps they might have been immortalized in her book. For who could visit Cross Creek without looking about for the characters which Mrs. Rawlings took from life and put boldly into her pages without consulting them or without even changing their names?

The characters in a novel are something else. You know they are products of the imagination, each perhaps a composite of many personalities which have been filtered through the author's mind. You know you will never encounter them in real life. But the characters in *Cross Creek* were real people. With libel laws being what they are, we are not likely to see another book like this one, dealing so candidly with the individuals of a community, describing them, quoting them, and discussing their varied ways of life in such a blatant invasion of privacy. You cannot imagine a publisher considering another *Cross Creek* without notarized releases signed by each character.

One of the characters in *Cross Creek,* Zelma Cason, did sue Mrs. Rawlings. Miss Cason, who appeared in the book as "my profane friend Zelma," charged that Mrs. Rawlings had stolen her personality and cheapened her name. A jury in Gainesville

Circuit Court, after hearing testimony that Miss Cason was as profane as she was characterized in *Cross Creek*, decided in favor of Mrs. Rawlings, but Miss Cason appealed to the Florida Supreme Court and won a reversal. The higher court decided that although Miss Cason had suffered "no mental anguish" (this conclusion is debatable) and therefore was entitled to no punitive damages, she had suffered a "wrongful invasion of privacy." At the higher court's direction, Circuit Judge A. M. Murphee of Gainesville awarded Miss Cason nominal damages—one dollar. It was an important victory for Miss Cason, because Mrs. Rawlings, the loser, had to pay court costs of $1,050, no small sum in the forties.

Although there was nothing intentionally derogatory in the way Mrs. Rawlings wrote about the people of Cross Creek, neither was any effort made to dress them up in garb and character they did not possess. Some came out pretty earthy. This, of course, was the reason for the book's popularity. It became a Book-of-the-Month selection and thousands of copies were sold. Readers recognized the faithful way Mrs. Rawlings had recorded life at Cross Creek, down to the very utterances—the actual words and phrases—used by the people who lived in this backcountry setting in the days before radio or television or modern schools.

The Rawlingses had discovered Cross Creek while searching for a picturesque but quiet rural community—a place with the kind of "atmosphere" that writers are always dreaming of. Both had worked on newspapers and both had sold enough articles and short stories to magazines to believe they could make a living from free-lancing. At Cross Creek they found a rambling cracker-style house in an orange grove set among tall cabbage palms, within view of Orange Lake. For a time they did quite well, selling enough of their writings and oranges to make a living. But the depression came and they could sell neither their writings nor citrus. Unable to make a living, Rawlings wanted to move. Mrs. Rawlings, however, refused to leave Cross Creek, and so they separated. He gave her the house and the grove and moved away. She buried herself in her writing.

"I just stuck to the typewriter for eight hours a day," she said later in recounting her years alone at Cross Creek. "I kept on working even if I turned out only two good lines a day."

Mrs. Rawlings, a native of Washington, D.C., was graduated from the University of Wisconsin. She had a nagging urge to write, but appeared to lack the temperament or the flair for newspaper work. In her early years her interest primarily was fiction and poetry, but although she worked tirelessly, she had written hardly anything of importance before coming to Florida. Then, after writing two less-than-fair novels and several short stories during her first decade at Cross Creek, she won a Pulitzer prize in 1939 for her third novel, *The Yearling.* She was forty-one. Three years later *Cross Creek* was published. It exploded in the community like a bomb.

Mrs. Pearl Glisson, who lives within hailing distance of the Rawlings home, remembers how upset some of the residents were. Miss Cason, who lived at nearby Island Grove, hastened over to see Mrs. Glisson's husband, Tom, a major character in the book.

"Zelma wanted to know what Tom aimed to do," recalled Mrs. Glisson. "She was very angry. But Tom said he didn't aim to do anything. He told Zelma:

" 'If Marge can come to Cross Creek and make a living writing about the people here, joy go with her.'

"But Zelma said she aimed to do something. 'I'm just not going to take it,' she said."

Mrs. Rawlings was surprised at the reaction, according to Mrs. Glisson.

"Marge thought that Zelma would be honored by the way she was quoted," said Mrs. Glisson.

Glisson died in 1950, Mrs. Rawlings in 1953, and Miss

Cason in 1963. Mrs. Glisson has the distinction of being one of the few Cross Creek residents of Mrs. Rawlings' period whose name do not appear in *Cross Creek.*

"I can't tell you why," she said. "Maybe it was because we always got along so well. It was my husband, Tom, that Marge had trouble with."

Mrs. Rawlings' bird dog, Mandy, died and someone told her that Tom Glisson had poisoned her. The difficulties between Mrs. Rawlings and Glisson which stemmed from this bit of evil gossip whispered into the author's ear is recounted at length in her book.

"The way Marge wrote it is a bit different from the way it actually happened," said Mrs. Glisson. "But I must say that in general what Marge wrote about Cross Creek was pretty close to the truth. I liked her writings, but I disapproved of the way she wrote about the underprivileged. I always thought that she must have hurt some of the people she mentioned—by the frank way she described them and quoted them."

Mrs. Glisson is well aware of the immortality of her husband's name as a character in *Cross Creek,* and she seems not to be unhappy about the way he comes to life in the pages. No photograph of Tom Glisson exists. An artist son of the Glissons tried to catch his likeness from memory, and the painting of a very strong, very determined man hangs in Mrs. Glisson's living room.

"That may not be the best possible likeness of Tom, but it has all of his strength," she said. "Tom was the only person who could handle Marge. She wasn't the easiest person in the world to get along with. Because we lived on adjoining properties, Marge and Tom had several spats. She would curse him when she got mad and when she learned that she was in the wrong she would cry."

Mrs. Glisson recounted the time Mrs. Rawlings fell out with Tom Glisson after the death of her bird dog.

"We knew something was wrong," she said, "but we couldn't find out what. Then one day Tom saw some of his hogs going into an open gate at Marge's home and he went down to run them out. Marge came out with a shotgun, and she started cursing Tom and accusing him of poisoning her dog. Tom went up to her and wrung the gun out of her hands and unloaded it. Then he came home. He was very angry.

"Later in the day we saw Marge coming down the road. I was afraid to let her in. Tom was so angry I thought he might hit her. I didn't want any trouble so I latched the door.

" 'Can I come in?' she asked when she found the door latched.

" 'No,' I said, 'you're wrong, Marge. We're not going to put up with this.'

"But Tom opened the door. 'Come on in,' he said.

"She came in and Tom said: 'I ought to take a chair and knock you out of this house.'

"She started crying and so did I.

" 'Tom,' she said, 'you are one of the best friends I've got. I want you to shake my hand and forget about what I accused you of.'

"But Tom wouldn't take her hand. He asked her who told her he had poisoned her dog. She said she had sworn not to tell. Tom called off several names. When he came to one name she butted in and said:

" 'Tom, let's stop all this. I've admitted that I was wrong. What good would it do if you knew who told me?'

"The tears were rolling down her face and her eyes were red. She and Tom finally shook hands and then Marge and me cried some more and after that everything was all right."

Mrs. Glisson remembers Mrs. Rawlings as a person who had strong likes and dislikes: "If she didn't like you she would tell you so. And when she was having one of her humors she could be cutting, even to her friends. There were times when she acted like she was carrying a chip on her shoulder. One day I said to her:

" 'Marge, what are you carrying a chip for?'

" 'I'm not carrying a chip,' she replied. 'When I'm writing I'm living in another world.' "

Mrs. Rawlings left her home and grove the the University of Florida. She hoped writers would find it a quiet and secluded place to work. But the curious came and bothered those who tried to work there and after awhile nobody used it. The university had no money to keep the place repaired or the grove maintained, and both began to deteriorate. Wild grasses that grew tall about the house died with the first frost and became tinder dry. A carelessly tossed match could have burned the house. Meanwhile, the house was invaded by "collectors" who carried away furniture, books, and even the curtains, as mementos.

"The people of Cross Creek were pretty bitter about the way the house was neglected," said Mrs. Glisson.

The University of Florida Foundation since has partially restored the house and had it painted. The house is now maintained as a museum by the state of Florida, and is open to the public every day except Mondays.

Two other prominent characters in *Cross Creek,* Snow Slater and his wife, the former Ella May Townsend, agreed that Mrs. Rawlings "embroidered the facts" a little in her writing.

"She was a wonderful person and I wouldn't want to say anything against her name," said Mrs. Slater, who reminded me that Mrs. Rawlings had given them the twelve-acre hammock site on Orange Lake, where they live in a small cottage at the end of a winding, sandy road. Slater was her grove caretaker. From Mrs. Slater I gained some insight into the way Mrs. Rawlings managed to get so close to the people at Cross Creek during the fifteen years between the time she came here and the time *Cross Creek* was published.

"She wore her clothes just like the rest of the people here," said Mrs. Slater. "You couldn't tell by looking at her whether she had any money. She wasn't a bit stuck-up. And she wasn't a tightwad, if you'll excuse the expression. At Christmas time she saw that Santa Claus came to the door of every poor child at Cross Creek.

"But things didn't always happen exactly the way she wrote about them. I know that a writer just has to change things a bit sometimes to make them sound right. Snow and I never bore any hard feelings against Mrs. Rawlings, though."

According to Slater, *Cross Creek* is 40 percent fact and 60 percent fiction.

"She could weave a fictional part to create a story," said Slater, who borrowed a pickup truck from Mrs. Rawlings to take his bride on a honeymoon to Gainesville in 1939. Mrs. Rawlings' account of the honeymoon in *Cross Creek* varies with the recollections of the Slaters. But Slater contends there is no fiction in Mrs. Rawlings description of Zelma Cason.

"You could hear Miss Cason cussing for a quarter of a mile," he said. "She was a small woman, maybe five feet four inches, but she cussed in a loud voice. She didn't care who heard her."

Slater recalled that there was only a sandy, rutty road to Cross Creek when the Rawlings arrived, and no electric power. They installed a Delco power plant, and its maintenance was one of Slater's jobs. His responsibilities increased after Rawlings departed. He not only had to maintain the grove, fertilizing and spraying the citrus trees, but harvested, packed, and sold the fruit. Like his wife, Slater was reluctant to discuss the disagreement between the Rawlingses which led to their separation. He was willing only to admit that disagreement existed and that Rawlings eventually departed.

George Fairbanks, who lives in a small shack on the Slater property, has never read *Cross Creek,* although he is one of the book's most colorful characters. Meeting the slender, weathered little man with his shock of wild, gray hair, was like rereading *Cross Creek*. He greeted me with the same nasal voice, the result of a cleft palate, that Mrs. Rawlings recorded when he came to her house to make courting overtures. At that time Mrs. Rawlings was living alone and so was Fairbanks. Moreover, his house had just burned. He was not a bit hesitant in suggesting that he and the author would make a good match.

"George was three sheets in the wind when he proposed to Mrs. Rawlings," suggested Snow Slater.

Fairbanks, seventy, lives on a small pension he receives from the state; since he never held a regular job he is not eligible for Social Security. The Fairbanks family at one time owned a fortune in orange groves and pinewoods about Cross Creek, but freezes wiped out the groves and the land went for taxes.

I found Fairbanks a delightful companion as he showed me about Cross Creek and guided me to Antioch Cemetery, nine miles distant, where Mrs. Rawlings is buried. Fairbanks pointed to another grave a short distance from where Mrs. Rawlings lies, that of Zelma Cason.

Fairbanks took out his makings and rolled a cigarette while I estimated the distance between the two almost identical granite slabs—seventy-five feet. The marker over Mrs. Rawlings' grave bears the name by which she was known to her reading public—"Marjorie Kinnan Rawlings. 1896-1953. Wife of Norton Baskins." Mrs. Rawlings and Baskins, the owner of a restaurant near Marineland, were married in the early forties.

"Through her writings," an inscription asserts, "she endeared herself to the people of the world."

More than half of the characters who will live forever in *Cross Creek* have passed on from actual life. Mrs. Rawlings' cook, Old Martha, died "four or five years ago," and her husband, Will Mickens, nearing his ninety-ninth birthday, lives with a daughter in nearby Hawthorne. I found Uncle Will, as he is known by blacks and whites alike, "uptown," sitting on the foot-worn steps of an old hardware store facing busy U.S. Highway 301. I sat with him in the warm December sunshine and his weathered old face lit up as we talked about Mrs. Rawlings.

"Lord, she was a vi'lent woman," he said. "She could cuss till the air turned blue—and she could cry; Lord, how that woman could cry."

Uncle Will shook his white head as he recalled an unforgettable day in the life of the author—the day she and her husband, Charles, went their separate ways.

"That was years back yonder, but I 'members it as if it was yestiddy—even though I be ninety-nine years old at noon tomorrow."

The homely philosophy and shrewd observations of Uncle Will's wife, Old Martha, appear throughout *Cross Creek*. Mickens is mentioned less frequently.

"The trouble was," Uncle Will continued, stretching out a cramped leg, "Mr. Charles, he wanted to go live by the water. But Missus Rawlings, she wanted to stay at Cross Creek. She say: 'I like it here and I ain't never gonna leave Cross Creek.' And Mr. Charles say: 'Well, I'm gonna go live by the water and if you wants to live with me you is gonna have to live by the water.'

"And round and round they go, on and on for days and days and ain't neither one giving in. They was times when I could smell 'shine on Mr. Charles' breath. He was a bothered man. But he was 'termined to go and live by the water."

Strings of traffic passed as Uncle Will spun his story. Big tractor-trailer trucks roared by, drowning his voice. But he kept talking. I could see his lips moving but could hear nothing except the roar of diesel motors.

"... And they went to town—to the bank at Gainesville—

and divided up all the money they had and they come back to Cross Creek where Mr. Charles packed his things and loaded them in his car.

" 'You can have the house and the land,' he said.

"She was crying and he was crying, and Old Martha was crying and I was crying. They shore was a lot of tears that day."

Uncle Will paused.

"I be ninety-nine at noon tomorrow," he repeated. "If I had a dime I'd go to the Cuba man and put it on that number —ninety-nine. But I ain't got no dime—and the Cuba books done closed anyhow."

Uncle Will tapped the thick wood steps with his walking cane.

"Missus Rawlings, she was a vi'lent woman. She was a woman with a mind of her own. She meant to stay at Cross Creek and she told her man that. 'But I'm gonna go live by the water,' Mr. Charles say as I helped him load his things in the car. . . . "

Another string of diesel trucks roared past. Uncle Will's lips moved but no audible sound issued from them until the trucks had passed.

". . . She was a vi'lent woman, sho' 'nough. One day I went to town with her and she knowed I was s'posed to buy Old Martha two pairs of stockings. Well, we was just starting back to Cross Creek when she say: 'Will, did you get Old Martha them stockings?' And I say: 'No'am, I ain't had 'nough money.' "

Uncle Will paused and looked about.

"Just wanted to see that they ain't no women folks in hearing distance," he said, then, leaning toward me, he whispered: "She say, 'Wil, you goddamned sorry nigger son-of-a-bitch!' She stopped the car right there in the middle of the street and she went in the sto' and bought Old Martha them stockings."

He paused, shook his head.

"But she warn't cussing none that day when Mr. Charles was fixing to leave Cross Creek. She was crying. All of us was crying. She say to Mr. Charles 'You go live by the water, but I'm gonna stay at Cross Creek and write.' The big tears rolls down her face and she had the snuffles.

"I 'members the last thing Mr. Charles say. He say: 'Marge, everything here at Cross Creek is yours—the house and the land, the grove.'

"Mr. Charles, he picked up his bird dog, Mandy, and held her in his arms—and he say: 'Marge, I'm a-giving you Mandy. You take good care of her.'

"And Mr. Charles, he handed Mandy to Missus Rawlings and he got in his car and driv' away . . . and there was the three of us a-standing there, with Missus Rawlings a-holding Mandy and the big tears a-rolling down her face . . . and Old Martha is crying and I is crying . . . and Missus Rawlings she say:

" 'Hell! Damn it to hell! Goddamn it to hell! '

"And all three of us cried some mo'."

Knights of the Fourth Estate

The Story of the Miami Herald

"An interesting and lively account of the *Miami Herald,* this work goes well beyond the usual insider's view of a newspaper. . . . The story of Miami is well narrated as a rich background to the account of the *Herald's* growth into a major newspaper." **Choice**

"The story of a metropolitan newspaper cannot be fully told unless the history of the area in which it flourished is told at the same time, a fact that Smiley acknowledges early and remains faithful to throughout. Smiley observes in his preface to this interesting history, 'Although *Knights of the Fourth Estate* is the story of the *Miami Herald,* it is also the story of Miami.' " **Inland Printer**

"Writing about living personalities with whom one has been closely allied can be tricky business for many writers. Smiley succeeds in creating a warm and believable portrait of John and Jim Knight, dignified and the ultimate in efficiency, but also capable of driving a hard bargain. Historians, students of the press in general, and admirers of the *Miami Herald* in particular will read this book with relish."

Richmond News Leader

341 pages, illustrated *cloth, $14.95*

Yesterday's Miami

"Newcomers will be awe-struck. Oldtimers will nod and smile at the memories of scenes long gone. Hardly anyone dipping into this gallery of 240 historical photographs will be able to put down the book before reading it from cover to cover. Smiley's words and choice of pictures trace the meteoric rise of Greater Miami over the past 75 years from a mosquito-infested swamp and palmetto scrub land into the subtropical metropolis of today. It is an exciting story, told in gripping form."

Miami Herald

E. A. SEEMANN PUBLISHING, INC., MIAMI, FLORIDA

Crowder Tales

"You expect a book like *Crowder Tales* to be corny because so many 'Tales'-type books from the rural South read like third-rate vaudeville. *Crowder Tales* is different. It's funny. Some of it is hilarious.

"Smiley grew up on a farm in a little swamp town on the Florida side of the Georgia state line with his grandparents; his uncle Scar; jivin' Jiggy Jat Joe; Peggy, the killer; a fraudulent Southern colonel; a non-selling salesman named Zenus; and a bunch of characters who are far too original to have been invented.

"I am not going to tell you a single story in the book. I can't. None will reduce to a couple of paragraphs. Smiley has to work up to everything. But the funniest story he tells is how old Colonel Higginbotham came to be buried alive, and how it affected Smiley's grandfather in his sleep after he had drunk a quart of whiskey."   **Southern Living**

169 pages with illustrations by Quin Hall   *cloth, $5.95*

Yesterday's Florida

Seemann's Historic States Series, No. 1

"Smiley has pulled together a collection of more than 500 photographs, drawings, and engravings relating to the history of Florida from the period of discovery and exploration to the present day. More than a judiciously chosen selection of pictures, the book also has a narrative commentary, and this, together with the detailed captions, make the work a major history of the state."   **Richmond News Leader**

"Smiley has produced a very attractive and interesting volumes which should be of value both to historians and to general readers. It is panoramic in concept and presentation. . . . He has produced an excellent volume. The book makes for easy reading, and one grasps from it a fresh and keen appreciation of Florida's history." **Georgia Historical Quarterly**

oversize format; 256 pages with 540 illustrations   *cloth, $12.95*

E. A. SEEMANN PUBLISHING, INC., MIAMI, FLORIDA

Lv Metro Rail
NW 79th St. + 37 Ave

1200 SW 11th Ave   TriRail

Lv TriRail   Enroute time = 1:10 to Del Ray
at 79th St. 1 pm →
        2:14
        3:25
        4:40